Larrie Benton Zacharie (Ed.)

Sport & Leisure Swifts F.C.

Larrie Benton Zacharie (Ed.)

Sport & Leisure Swifts F.C.

IFA, Championship, Northern, Irish, Football, Club, Sport

VerPublishing

Imprint

Permission is granted to copy, distribute and/or modify this document under the terms of the GNU Free Documentation License, Version 1.2 or any later version published by the Free Software Foundation; with no Invariant Sections, with the Front-Cover Texts, and with the Back- Cover Texts. A copy of the license is included in the section entitled "GNU Free Documentation License".

All parts of this book are extracted from Wikipedia, the free encyclopedia (www.wikipedia.org).

You can get detailed informations about the authors of this collection of articles at the end of this book. The editors (Ed.) of this book are no authors. They have not modified or extended the original texts.

Pictures published in this book can be under different licences than the GNU Free Documentation License. You can get detailed informations about the authors and licences of pictures at the end of this book.

The content of this book was generated collaboratively by volunteers. Please be advised that nothing found here has necessarily been reviewed by people with the expertise required to provide you with complete, accurate or reliable information. Some information in this book maybe misleading or wrong. The Publisher does not guarantee the validity of the information found here. If you need specific advice (f.e. in fields of medical, legal, financial, or risk management questions) please contact a professional who is licensed or knowledgeable in that area.

Any brand names and product names mentioned in this book are subject to trademark, brand or patent protection and are trademarks or registered trademarks of their respective holders. The use of brand names, product names, common names, trade names, product descriptions etc. even without a particular marking in this works is in no way to be construed to mean that such names may be regarded as unrestricted in respect of trademark and brand protection legislation and could thus be used by anyone.

Cover image: www.ingimage.com
Concerning the licence of the cover image please contact ingimage.

Publisher:
VerPublishing is a trademark of
International Book Market Service Ltd., 17 Rue Meldrum, Beau Bassin, 1713-01 Mauritius
Email: info@bookmarketservice.com
Website: www.bookmarketservice.com

Published in 2012

Printed in: U.S.A., U.K., Germany. This book was not produced in Mauritius.

ISBN: 978-613-8-77854-7

Contents

Articles

Sport_&_Leisure_Swifts_F.C.	1
IFA_Championship	2
Northern_Amateur_Football_League	9
Inver_Park	23
Chimney_Corner_F.C.	24
Allen_Park,_Michigan	26
Antrim,_County_Antrim	30
Association_football_in_Northern_Ireland	35
IFA_Premiership	37
Association_football	50

References

Article Sources and Contributors	63
Image Sources, Licenses and Contributors	65

Sport_&_Leisure_Swifts_F.C.

Full name	Sport & Leisure Swifts Football Club
Founded	1978
Ground	Glen Road Heights, Belfast
2010/11	8th

Sport & Leisure Swifts F.C. is an intermediate, Northern Irish football club playing in IFA Championship 2. The club hails from Belfast. It was founded in 1978 and played in the County Down Premier League and the Dunmurry League, before joining the Northern Amateur League in 1990.[1]

The club joined the IFA Championship in 2009. It shared Larne's Inver Park ground while its own home at Glen Road was improved to Championship standard.[2]

History

Sport & Leisure F.C. was founded in 1978 when a group of players approached a local Belfast businessman to provide kit for their new team and he agreed, with the proviso that his company name, Ulster Sport & Leisure Club, appeared on the shirts. The club adopted the name "Sport & Leisure", which remains to this day, despite the disappearance of the original business. The name "Swifts" was added when a number of players from Dunmurry League side **Belfast Swifts F.C.** left to join Sport & Leisure.[3]

Admittance to the Amateur League was dependent the club having its own pitch, and this was achieved in 1990, when Chimney Corner's ground Allen Park, Antrim, was made available. The club acquired the use of Larkfield High School's ground in Belfast in 1991, before opening its own ground at Glen Road Heights in 2001.[4]

In 2003, intermediate status was achieved.[5]

External links

- Official Club Website [6]
- The Ulster Groundhop [7]

References

[1] H. Johnstone & G. Hamilton (n.d.) *A Memorable Milestone: 75 Years of the Northern Amateur Football League*, p. 218
[2] Club details (http://www.sportandleisureswifts.co.uk/)
[3] "Swiftly Does It", *NI Football*, p.38, Issue 16, Winter 2010. Belfast:Irish Football Association
[4] "Swiftly Does It", *NI Football*, p.38, Issue 16, Winter 2010. Belfast:Irish Football Association
[5] "Swiftly Does It", *NI Football*, p.38, Issue 16, Winter 2010. Belfast:Irish Football Association
[6] http://www.sportandleisureswifts.co.uk/
[7] http://www.youtube.com/watch?v=3BmYTqHiXZM

IFA_Championship

Countries	Northern Ireland
Founded	2008 2004–2008 (*as IFA Intermediate League First Division*) 2003–2004 (*as Irish League First Division*) 1999–2003 (*as Irish League Second Division*) 1977–1999 (as Irish League B Division Section 1) 1951–1977 (*as Irish League B Division*)
Number of teams	30 (two divisions)
Levels on pyramid	2 and 3
Promotion to	IFA Premiership
Relegation to	Ballymena & Provincial Intermediate League Mid-Ulster Football League Northern Amateur League Northern Ireland Intermediate League
Domestic cup(s)	Irish Cup Irish League Cup IFA Intermediate Cup
Current champions	Carrick Rangers (2010–11)
	2011–12 IFA Championship

The **IFA Championship** is a football league in Northern Ireland. It is one level below the IFA Premiership, which is Northern Ireland's national league. Clubs in the Championship have intermediate status.

It was founded in 2008 to succeed the **IFA Intermediate League** which folded as part of the reorganisation of top-level football in Northern Ireland that saw the creation of stricter entry criteria in respect of the newly-established Premiership and Championship. In 2009, it was extended to two divisions: **Championship 1** and **Championship 2** with promotion and relegation between the two.[1] . The Championship is sponsored by the Belfast Telegraph and is marketed as the **Belfast Telegraph Championship**.[2] 'IFA' refers to the Irish Football Association.

Results from Championship 1 are featured on the Press Association vidiprinter service. However, they are rarely seen by television viewers as the Saturday results often do not appear until after 5.15pm and therefore are not featured during the reading of the classified results. The results from Championship 2 are not carried on the Press Association vidiprinter service.

History

The IFA Championship is the successor to the **IFA Intermediate League**, the **Irish Football League First Division** during its last season (when it had intermediate status), and ultimately the **Irish League B Division** (latterly known as the **Irish League Second Division**).

The **B Division** of the Irish League was founded in 1951, and originally consisted of the reserve teams of the senior Irish League clubs alongside some of the top intermediate clubs. The B Division was split geographically into North and South sections in 1974 (with a play-off to determine the winners in 1974–75 and 1975–76), and then into **Section 1** (containing the intermediate clubs) and **Section 2** (the reserve teams of senior clubs) in 1977.

In 1999, the B Division Section 1 was renamed as the **Irish League Second Division**, and Section 2 became the **Reserve League**.

There was never any automatic promotion and relegation between either the B Division or Second Division and the senior Irish League.

In 2003, the Irish Premier League was formed by the top sixteen senior teams in the senior Irish League (which, since 1995 had been divided into a Premier Division and a First Division). The four remaining senior teams reverted to intermediate football, along with the top eight teams from the previous year's Second Division - in the Irish League First Division (which now became the top intermediate league), with the Second Division continuing with twelve teams. Automatic promotion and relegation between senior and intermediate football was introduced for the first time. There was also automatic promotion and relegation between the two divisions of the (now intermediate-status) Irish League.

In 2004, the Irish Football League was wound up and replaced by the **IFA Intermediate League**, consisting of two divisions of twelve, with promotion and relegation between the two. This continued for four seasons, until the Championship was created.

For one season only, 2008–09, there was also an IFA Interim Intermediate League for those former members of the IFA Intermediate League which had failed to meet the criteria for the Championship. These clubs were given a year to make improvements in order to join the Championship for 2009–10. Ten of the 12 clubs succeeded in meeting the necessary standard in 2009 and the Championship was then divided into two divisions.

As of 2010–11, a "pyramid" system has been introduced in Northern Ireland, with the possibility of promotion and relegation between the Championship and the four regional intermediate leagues, namely:

- **Ballymena & Provincial Intermediate League**
- **Mid-Ulster Football League**
- **Northern Amateur League**
- **Northern Ireland Intermediate League**

Clubs in these leagues may only gain promotion to the Championship if they win their respective league championship and meet the necessary criteria. In the event that more than one league champion meets the criteria, only one will be promoted, to be decided by a play-off or series of play-offs.

Current Championship clubs (2011–12)

Championship 1
- Ards
- Ballinamallard United
- Banbridge Town
- Bangor
- Dergview
- Glebe Rangers
- Harland & Wolff Welders
- Institute
- Larne
- Limavady United
- Loughgall
- Newry City
- Tobermore United
- Warrenpoint Town

Championship 2
- Annagh United
- Armagh City
- Ballyclare Comrades
- Ballymoney United
- Chimney Corner
- Coagh United
- Dundela
- Killymoon Rangers
- Knockbreda
- Lurgan Celtic
- Moyola Park
- Portstewart
- PSNI
- Queen's University Belfast
- Sport & Leisure Swifts
- Wakehurst

List of champions

Season	Champions	Second-level champions
Irish League B Division		
1951–52	Linfield Swifts[3]	n/a
1952–53	Linfield Swifts[3]	n/a
1953–54	Cliftonville Olympic[3]	n/a
1954–55	Larne	n/a
1955–56	Banbridge Town	n/a
1956–57	Larne	n/a
1957–58	Ards II[3]	n/a
1958–59	Glentoran II[3]	n/a
1959–60	Newry Town[4]	n/a
1960–61	Ballyclare Comrades	n/a
1961–62	Carrick Rangers	n/a
1962–63	Ballyclare Comrades	n/a
1963–64	Larne	n/a
1964–65	Larne	n/a
1965–66	Larne	n/a
1966–67	Larne	n/a
1967–68	Dundela	n/a
1968–69	Larne	n/a
1969–70	Larne	n/a
1970–71	Larne	n/a

1971–72	Larne†	n/a
1972–73	Carrick Rangers	n/a
1973–74	Ballyclare Comrades	n/a
1974–75	Carrick Rangers [5]	n/a
1975–76	Linfield Swifts [3][5]	n/a
1976–77	Carrick Rangers / Dundela[6]	n/a
Irish League B Division Section 1		
1977–78	Ballyclare Comrades	n/a
1978–79	Carrick Rangers	n/a
1979–80	Ballyclare Comrades	n/a
1980–81	Newry Town[4]	n/a
1981–82	Dundela	n/a
1982–83	Carrick Rangers†	n/a
1983–84	Limavady United	n/a
1984–85	Chimney Corner	n/a
1985–86	Dundela	n/a
1986–87	RUC[7]	n/a
1987–88	Dundela	n/a
1988–89	Ballyclare Comrades	n/a
1989–90	Dundela	n/a
1990–91	Dundela	n/a
1991–92	Dundela	n/a
1992–93	Limavady United	n/a
1993–94	Dundela	n/a
1994–95	Loughgall	n/a
1995–96	Loughgall	n/a
1996–97	Loughgall	n/a
1997–98	Loughgall	n/a
1998–99	Chimney Corner	n/a
Irish League Second Division		
1999–00	Dundela	n/a
2000–01	Dundela	n/a
2001–02	Moyola Park	n/a
2002–03	Ballinamallard United	n/a
Irish League		
2003–04	Loughgall‡	Coagh United
IFA Intermediate League		
2004–05	Armagh City‡	Tobermore United

2005–06	Crusaders‡	Portstewart
2006–07	Institute‡	Ballyclare Comrades
2007–08	Loughgall	Dergview
	IFA Championship	
2008–09	Portadown‡	n/a
2009–10	Loughgall	Harland & Wolff Welders
2010–11	Carrick Rangers‡	Warrenpoint Town

† Elected to senior Irish Football League
‡ Promoted to Irish Premier League/IFA Premiership

Summary of champions

	Team	Wins	Last win
1	Dundela	11[8]	2000–01
2	Larne	10	1971–72
3	Carrick Rangers	7[8]	2010–11
=	Loughgall	7	2009–10
5	Ballyclare Comrades	6	1988–89
6	Linfield Swifts	3	1975–76
7	Chimney Corner	2	1998–99
=	Limavady United	2	1992–93
=	Newry City [9]	2	1980–81
10	Ards II	1	1957–58
=	Armagh City	1	2004–05
=	Ballinamallard United	1	2002–03
=	Banbridge Town	1	1955–56
=	Cliftonville Olympic	1	1953–54
=	Crusaders	1	2005–06
=	Glentoran II	1	1958–59
=	Institute	1	2006–07
=	Moyola Park	1	2001–02
=	PSNI[10]	1	1986–87
=	Portadown	1	2008–09

Knock-out competitions

In 1982, a knock-out competition for members was introduced, known as the **B Division Knock-out Cup** and sponsored by Smirnoff. It was discontinued after 2002, but a new **IFA Intermediate League Cup** was played between 2004 and 2008, sponsored in its first season by the *Daily Mirror* and thereafter by Carnegie. In 2008–09, there was no knock-out competition for Championship clubs, who participated with Premiership clubs in the Irish League Cup. For 2009–10, however, while Championship 1 clubs continued to participate in the Irish League Cup, a **Championship 2 League Cup** was inaugurated for those in Championship 2. From 2010–11, Championship 2 clubs also competed in the Irish League Cup, and there was no separate league cup for the Championship.

Winners

Season	Winners
B Division Knock-out Cup	
1982–83	R.U.C.
1983–84	Ballyclare Comrades
1984–85	R.U.C.
1985–86	R.U.C.
1986–87	Chimney Corner
1987–88	Dundela
1988–89	Ballyclare Comrades
1989–90	Omagh Town
1990–91	Dundela
1991–92	Dundela
1992–93	Limavady United
1993–94	Dungannon Swifts
1994–95	Dundela
1995–96	Limavady United
1996–97	Institute
1997–98	Harland & Wolff Welders
1998–99	Ballymoney United
1999–00	Moyola Park
2000–01	Harland & Wolff Welders
2001–02	Harland & Wolff Welders
2002–03	*no competition*
2003–04	*no competition*
IFA Intermediate League Cup	
2004–05	Bangor
2005–06	Crusaders
2006–07	Institute
2007–08	Loughgall
2008–09	*no competition*

Championship 2 League Cup	
2009–10	Harland & Wolff Welders[11]
2010–11	*no competition*

Summary of winners

	Team	Wins	Last win
1	Dundela	4	1994–95
=	Harland & Wolff Welders	4	2009–10
3	R.U.C.[7]	3	1985–86
4	Ballyclare Comrades	2	1988–89
=	Institute	2	2006–07
=	Limavady United	2	1995–96
6	Ballymoney United	1	1998–99
=	Bangor	1	2004–05
=	Chimney Corner	1	1986–87
=	Crusaders	1	2005–06
=	Dungannon Swifts	1	1993–94
=	Loughgall	1	2007–08
=	Moyola Park	1	1999–00
=	Omagh Town	1	1989–90

See also

- IFA Premiership
- IFA Interim Intermediate League
- IFA Reserve League
- IFA Intermediate Cup
- Irish Cup
- Irish Football League Cup
- County Antrim Shield
- Steel & Sons Cup
- Mid-Ulster Cup
- Bob Radcliffe Cup
- North West Senior Cup
- Craig Memorial Cup
- Northern Ireland football league system

References

[1] Ladbrokes.com Championship 2009/10 (http://www.ifachampionship.com/news020709_1.htm)
[2] BELFAST TELEGRAPH SPONSOR THE IFA CHAMPIONSHIP (http://www.irishfa.com/news/item/6851/belfast-telegraph-sponsor-the-ifa-championship/)
[3] Reserve team of senior club
[4] Now Newry City
[5] After play-off between winners of North and South sections
[6] Shared between winners of North and South sections
[7] Now PSNI
[8] Including one shared title
[9] As Newry Town
[10] As RUC
[11] Welders lift League Cup (http://www.ifachampionship.com/news160310_1.htm)

General

- Malcolm Brodie (ed.), *Northern Ireland Soccer Yearbook* (various editions)

Notes

Northern_Amateur_Football_League

The **Northern Amateur Football League**, also known as the **Northern Amateur League** and often simply as the **Amateur League**, is an association football league in Northern Ireland. It contains 13 divisions. These comprise four intermediate sections: the Premier Division, Division 1A, Division 1B and Division 1C; three junior sections: Division 2A, Division 2B and Division 2C; and six reserve sections.

Clubs in membership (2011-12)

Premier Division	Division 1A	Division 1B	Division 1C
Albert Foundry	Abbey Villa	Ballynahinch United	1st Bangor Old Boys
Ards Rangers	Ardglass	Ballywalter Recreation	18th Newtownabbey Old Boys
Comber Recreation	Barn United	Bangor Rangers	Bangor Amateurs
Downpatrick	Crumlin United	Bryansburn Rangers	Bangor Swifts
Dromara Village	Derriaghy Cricket Club	Crumlin Star	Bloomfield
Dunmurry Recreation	Drumaness Mills	Donard Hospital	Civil Service
Islandmagee	Dundonald	Downshire Young Men	Dromore Amateurs
Killyleagh Youth	East Belfast	Dunmurry Young Men	Groomsport
Kilmore Recreation	Grove United	Lisburn Rangers	Immaculata
Malachians	Holywood	Newcastle	Iveagh United
Newington Youth Club	Larne Technical Old Boys	Orangefield Old Boys	Kilroot Rec.
Nortel	Saintfield United	Rathfern Rangers	Mossley Young Men
Rosario Youth Club	U.U.J.	Rathfriland Rangers	Newington Rangers
Shankill United	Wellington Recreation	Sirocco Works	Short Brothers

Format

The league season lasts from August to May with each club playing the others twice, once at their home ground and once at that of their opponents. Teams receive three points for a win and one point for a draw. No points are awarded for a loss. Teams are ranked by total points, then goal difference, and then goals scored. At the end of each season, the team that finishes in first place in the Premier division is crowned league champions.

Premier Division

There are 14 clubs in the Premier Division, each playing a total of 26 games. The two lowest-placed teams are relegated to Division 1A.

Division 1A

There are 14 clubs. The two highest-placed teams are promoted into the Premier Division whilst the two lowest-placed teams are relegated to Division 1B.

Division 1B

There are 14 clubs. The two highest-placed teams are promoted to Division 1A and the two lowest-placed teams are relegated to Division 1C.

Division 1C

This division was added to the Amateur League for the 2009/10 season. It now consists of 14 teams who will each play a total of 26 matches. The two top-placed teams at the end of the season will be promoted to Division 1B.

Second Division

There are three sections within the Second Division, which has junior status: Division 2A, Division 2B and Division 2C. The top team in Division 2A at the end of the season can be promoted into the Intermediate section as long as their grounds meet intermediate standards.

Third Division

The Third Division is for reserve sides of teams in the first and second divisions. It has six sections: 3A to 3F.

Cup competitions

There are two cup competitions at intermediate level: the **Border Regiment Cup**, more commonly referred to as the **Border Cup**, the final of which is played during the Christmas period, is a knock-out competition for First Division clubs. The **Clarence Cup** is a knock-out competition for all clubs (encompassing both the First and Second Divisions).

History

The League was founded 4th July 1923 at a meeting of fourteen clubs at the Clarence Place Hall, Donegall Square East, Belfast, initially as a league for teams from public bodies, private associations, schools and firms. It was affiliated to the Irish Football Association as a junior league in August. The first season was 1923/24 and by the time the first fixtures were played on 22nd September, there were 16 member clubs. The Co-operative and C.P.A. were tied at the top of the table, but the Co-operative won a play-off to be crowned the first Amateur League champions.

A knock-out competition - the **Clarence Cup** - was also inaugurated in the first season, and the first winners were C.P.A., who beat the Co-operative 2-1 in a replay after a 0-0 draw.

The League's first representative game was played on 26th January 1924 against the Minor League at the Oval, and was a 6-1 win for the Amateur League. In 1932, the League played its first representative match outside Northern Ireland: a 3-3 draw against the Scottish Juvenile FA at Celtic Park, Glasgow. This became an annual fixture, which lasted until 1939, only to be halted by the Second World War. Subsequently, annual fixtures have resumed, first with the Scottish Amateur League and, since 1978-79 with the Scottish Amateur F.A., competing for the **Britton Rosebowl**.

During the next few years, the League gained intermediate status, and a junior-status second division was added in 1926. By 1930, there were 30 clubs in membership. In 1932-33, the League's strength was demonstrated when Dunville's became the first Amateur League team to win the Irish Intermediate Cup, and in 1938-39 when Sirocco Works won the Steel & Sons Cup.

In the 1936-37 season, a new competition was introduced: the **Border Regiment Cup** (commonly the **Border Cup**), which was to become the perhaps League's most prestigious trophy as it established a traditional Christmas final. The cup was presented to the league by the team of the Border Regiment, stationed at Palace Barracks, Holywood, which had been a member of the League since 1933, and which was nearing the end of its tour of duty. The first winners were Sirocco Works, who beat Whitehouse Recreation Club 4-0 in the final.

After the Second World War, the league expanded its membership and the second division was split into two - Division 2A and Division 2B - in 1947. Division 2C was added in 1950. In 1961, Division 2A was elevated to intermediate status as Division 1B, with the top division renamed as Division 1A. Divisions 2B and 2C consequently became 2A and 2B respectively. The next year, 1962, the league expanded again and a new Division 2C was added, making a total of five divisions.

In 1963, it was decided that the Border Cup should be confined to teams in the First Division, and a new knock-out competition - the **Cochrane Corry Cup** - was instituted for the Second Division teams.

From the 1970-71 season, automatic promotion and relegation within each division was introduced, and in the following season a new Third Division was added for the reserve teams of member clubs. In 1971 Division 2C was abolished, but re-established again in 1975. In 1973 a second reserve section was formed and the Third Division was thus divided into Division 3A and Division 3B. Division 3C was added in 1980, Division 3D in 1986 and Division 3E in 1991. There is now a Division 3F.

The League had been growing, particularly since the 1960s, and the milestone of 100 teams in membership was achieved in 1981. (By 1997-98, there were 144 teams in membership.) In 1985, the League secured a sponsorship deal with Smithwick's.

In 1986, the intermediate First Division was expanded into three sections with the addition of Division 1C. From 1991 the intermediate sections were renamed as the Premier Division, Division 1A and Division 1B. Minimum standards were set for clubs' grounds as a condition of membership of the Premier Division, with promotion only available to those clubs whose facilities measured up.

List of champions

Season	Winner
1923/24	Co-operative
1924/25	N.C.C.
1925/26	N.C.C.
1926/27	Sirocco Works
1927/28	Shaftesbury
1928/29	Shaftesbury
1929/30	Holm Factory
1930/31	Dunville's
1931/32	Dunville's
1932/33	Dunville's
1933/34	Dunville's
1934/35	Sirocco Works
1935/36	Sirocco Works
1936/37	Sirocco Works
1937/38	Sirocco Works
1938/39	Sirocco Works
1939/40	Sirocco Works
1940/41	Victoria Works
1941/42	Victoria Works United
1942/43	Victoria Works United
1943/44	Shankill Young Men
1944/45	Shankill Young Men
1945/46	Shankill Young Men
1946/47	Queen's Island Woodworkers
1947/48	Sirocco Works
1948/49	Carrick Rangers
1949/50	East Belfast
1950/51	Musgrave
1951/52	Carrick Rangers
1952/53	East Belfast
1953/54	East Belfast
1954/55	East Belfast
1955/56	East Belfast
1956/57	Short Brothers & Harland
1957/58	Short Brothers & Harland
1958/59	Short Brothers & Harland
1959/60	Short Brothers & Harland
1960/61	Albert Foundry[1]

1961/62	Chimney Corner
1962/63	East Belfast
1963/64	East Belfast
1964/65	St Elizabeth's
1965/66	East Belfast
1966/67	Albert Foundry
1967/68	Islandmagee
1968/69	Chimney Corner
1969/70	Chimney Corner
1970/71	R.U.C.
1971/72	I.C.L.
1972/73	R.U.C.
1973/74	Chimney Corner
1974/75	Chimney Corner
1975/76	Barn United
1976/77	Downpatrick Rec.
1977/78	Downpatrick Rec.
1978/79	Harland & Wolff Welders
1979/80	Dunmurry Rec.
1980/81	Downpatrick Rec.
1981/82	Drumaness Mills
1982/83	S.T.C.
1983/84	Drumaness Mills
1984/85	Killyleagh Youth
1985/86	Cromac Albion
1986/87	Cromac Albion
1987/88	Dunmurry Rec.
1988/89	Drumaness Mills
1989/90	Short Brothers
1990/91	Harland & Wolff Sports
1991/92	Dunmurry Rec.
1992/93	Killyleagh Youth
1993/94	East Belfast
1994/95	Crumlin United
1995/96	Northern Telecom
1996/97	Northern Telecom
1997/98	Ards Rangers
1998/89	Dunmurry Rec.
1999/2000	Killyleagh Youth

Season	Winner
2000/01	Killyleagh Youth
2001/02	Killyleagh Youth
2002/03	Killyleagh Youth
2003/04	Killyleagh Youth
2004/05	Killyleagh Youth
2005/06	Newington Youth Club
2006/07	Albert Foundry[2]
2007/08	Downpatrick
2008/09	Newington Youth Club
2009/10	Newington Youth Club
2010/11	Newington Youth Club

Performance by club

	Team	Wins	Last win
1	East Belfast	9	1993/94
2	Killyleagh Youth	8	2004/05
=	Sirocco Works	8	1947/48
4	Dunville's**	6	1933/34
5	Chimney Corner	5	1974/75
=	Short Brothers†	5	1989/90
7	Dunmurry Rec.	4	1998/99
=	Newington Youth Club	4	2010/11
9	Downpatrick Rec.	3	1980/81
=	Drumaness Mills	3	1988/89
=	Nortel‡	3	1996/97
=	Shankill Young Men	3	1945/46
=	Victoria Works United*	3	1942/43
14	Carrick Rangers	2	1951/52
=	Cromac Albion	2	1986/87
=	N.C.C.	2	1925/26
=	R.U.C.	2	1972/73
18	Albert Foundry (1)	2	1960/61
=	Ards Rangers	1	1997/98
=	Barn United	1	1923/24
=	Co-operative	1	1923/24
=	Crumlin United	1	1994/95
=	Downpatrick	1	2007/08
=	Harland & Wolff Welders	1	1978/79

=	Harland & Wolff Sports	1	1990/91
=	Islandmagee	1	1967/68
=	Musgrave	1	1950/51
=	Holm Factory	1	1929/30
=	I.C.L.	1	1971/72
=	Queen's Island Woodworkers	1	1946/47
=	St Elizabeth's	1	1964/65

* Including one as Victoria Works.

** Including two as Shaftesbury.

† Including four as Short Brothers & Harland.

‡ One as S.T.C. and two as Northern Telecom.

List of Clarence Cup winners

Season	Winner
1923/24	C.P.A.
1924/25	Ophir
1925/26	Sirocco Works
1926/27	Sirocco Works
1927/28	Shaftesbury
1928/29	Shaftesbury
1929/30	Shaftesbury
1930/31	Dunville's
1931/32	Ewarts
1932/33	Cliftonville Strollers
1933/34	49th (Scouts) Old Boys
1934/35	Border Regiment
1935/36	Willowfield
1936/37	Whitehouse Rec.
1937/38	Whitehouse Rec.
1938/39	Sirocco Works
1939/40	Aircraft Works II
1940/41	Victoria Works
1941/42	Victoria Works United
1942/43	Victoria Works United
1943/44	Sirocco Works
1944/45	Shankill Young Men
1945/46	Sirocco Works
1946/47	East Belfast
1947/48	Sirocco Works

1948/49	Cogry Mills
1949/50	East Belfast
1950/51	East Belfast
1951/52	East Belfast
1952/53	Wolfhill Rec.
1953/54	Balmoral Rec.
1954/55	Balmoral R.C.
1955/56	Chimney Corner
1956/57	East Belfast
1957/58	Comber Rec.
1958/59	Ewarts
1959/60	Harland & Wolff S.M.D.
1960/61	R.U.C.
1961/62	Comber Rec.
1962/63	Bethel Young Men
1963/64	Albert Foundry[1]
1964/65	Lisburn Rangers
1965/66	St Elizabeth's
1966/67	Albert Foundry[1]
1967/68	Dundonald
1968/69	Harland & Wolff Welders 'A'
1969/70	Chimney Corner
1970/71	*Cup withheld*[3]
1971/72	R.N.A.Y.
1972/73	Lisburn Rangers
1973/74	S.T.C.
1974/75	Downpatrick Rec.
1975/76	Barn United
1976/77	Balmoral Rec.
1977/78	Cromac Albion
1978/79	Downpatrick Rec.
1979/80	Cromac Albion
1980/81	Ballyclare Comrades Reserves
1981/82	Civil Service
1982/83	Ballyclare Comrades Reserves
1983/84	Ballyclare Comrades Reserves
1984/85	Carreras Rothmans
1985/86	S.T.C.
1986/87	Harland & Wolff Sports

Season	Winner
1987/88	Grove United
1988/89	Harland & Wolff Sports
1989/90	Rooftop
1990/91	Abbey Villa
1991/92	Harland & Wolff Sports
1992/93	Drumaness Mills
1993/94	Drumaness Mills
1994/95	Barn United
1995/96	*Cup withheld*[4]
1996/97	Ballynahinch United
1997/98	Killyleagh Youth
1998/99	Comber Rec.
1999/2000	?
2000/01	Killyleagh Youth
2001/02	Killyleagh Youth
2002/03	Bangor Amateurs
2003/04	Kilmore Rec.
2004/05	Kilmore Rec.
2005/06	Barn United
2006/07	East Belfast
2007/08	Islandmagee
2008/09	Immaculata
2009/10	Albert Foundry
2010/11	Immaculata

Performance by club

	Team	Wins	Last win
1	Sirocco Works	6	1947/48
=	East Belfast	6	2006/07
3	Dunville's*	4	1930/31
4	Albert Foundry[1]	3	2009/10
=	Ballyclare Comrades Reserves	3	1983/84
=	Balmoral Rec.	3	1976/77
=	Barn United	3	2005/06
=	Comber Rec.	3	1999/2000
=	Harland & Wolff Sports	3	1991/92
=	Killyleagh Youth	3	2001/02
=	Victoria Works United**	3	1942/43

12	Chimney Corner	2	1969/70
=	Cromac Albion	2	1979/80
=	Downpatrick Rec.	2	1978/79
=	Drumaness Mills	2	1993/94
=	Ewarts	2	1958/59
=	Immaculata	2	2010/11
=	Kilmore Rec.	2	2004/05
=	Lisburn Rangers	2	1972/73
=	S.T.C.	2	1985/86
=	Whitehouse R.C.	2	1937/38
23	49th (Scouts) Old Boys	1	1933/34
=	Abbey Villa	1	1990/91
=	Aircraft Works II	1	1939/40
=	Ballynahinch United	1	1996/97
=	Bangor Amateurs	1	2002/03
=	Bethel Young Men	1	1962/63
=	Border Regiment	1	1934/35
=	C.P.A.	1	1923/24
=	Carreras Rothmans	1	1984/85
=	Civil Service	1	1981/82
=	Cogry Mills	1	1948/49
=	Cliftonville Strollers	1	1932/33
=	Dundonald	1	1967/68
=	Grove United	1	1987/88
=	Harland & Wolff S.M.D.	1	1959/60
=	Harland & Wolff Welders 'A'	1	1968/69
=	Islandmagee	1	2007/08
=	Ophir	1	1924/25
=	R.N.A.Y.	1	1971/72
=	Rooftop	1	1989/90
=	R.U.C.	1	1960/61
=	St Elizabeth's	1	1965/66
=	Shankill Young Men	1	1944/45
=	Willowfield	1	1935/36
=	Wolfhill Rec.	1	1952/53

* Including three as Shaftesbury.

** Including one as Victoria Works.

List of Border Cup winners

Season	Winner	Score	Score	Runner-up	Notes
1936/37	Sirocco Works	4	0	Whitehouse Recreation	
1937/38	Sirocco Works				
1938/39	Sirocco Works				
1939/40					
1940/41					
1941/42	Sirocco Works				
1942/43					
1943/44					
1944/45	Sirocco Works				
1945/46	Sirocco Works				
1946/47					
1947/48					
1948/49					
1949/50	Albert Foundry				
1950/51					
1951/52					
1952/53					
1953/54	Dunmurry Rec				
1954/55					
1955/56					
1956/57	Comber Rec			Chimney Corner	
1957/58	Comber Rec			Short Brothers & Harlands	
1958/59					
1959/60					
1960/61	Albert Foundry				
1961/62					
1962/63	Albert Foundry				
1963/64				Albert Foundry	
1964/65	RUC			Islandmagee	
1965/66	Islandmagee	1	0	Albert Foundry	
1966/67	Ards Rangers				
1967/68	Chimney Corner	3	1	Islandmagee	
1968/69					
1969/70				Albert Foundry	
1970/71					
1971/72					
1972/73					

1973/74						
1974/75	Chimney Corner	1	0	STC		
1975/76	Larne Tech Old Boys					
1976/77						
1977/78	Drumaness Mills					
1978/79	Drumaness Mills					
1979/80	Ards Rangers			Larne Tech Old Boys		
1980/81	Drumaness Mills					
1981/82	Ballynahinch United			British Telecom		
1982/83	STC					
1983/84						
1984/85						
1985/86	STC			Sirocco Works		
1986/87	Drumaness Mills					
1987/88						
1988/89						
1989/90						
1990/91	STC			Bangor Amateurs		
1991/92	Dunmurry Rec.			East Belfast		
1992/93	Abbey Villa	5	0	Drumaness Mills		
1993/94	?(FC Enkalon or 1st Liverpool RR?)					
1994/95	1st Shankill Northern Ireland Supporters Club	3	1	Islandmagee		
1995/96	Coagh United	3	3	Islandmagee	Coagh won 4-2 on penalties	
1996/97	Killyleagh Youth					
1997/98	Larne Technical Old Boys					
1998/99	Islandmagee	3	1	Killyleagh Youth		
1999/2000	Northern Telecom	2	0	Ards Rangers		
2000/01	Crumlin United			Drumaness Mills		
2001/02	Larne Technical Old Boys					
2002/03	Killyleagh Youth	2	0	Kilmore Rec		
2003/04	Killyleagh Youth	2	1	Downpatrick		
2004/05	Knockbreda Parish			Albert Foundry		
2005/06	Newington Y.C.					
2006/07	Dunmurry Rec.	3	0	Kilmore Rec	[5]	
2007/08	Abbey Villa	3	2	Comber Rec		
2008/09	Sport & Leisure Swifts	3	1	Kilmore Rec	[6]	
2009/10	Grove United	1	1	Dromara Village	Grove won 7-6 on penalties[7]	
2010/11	Dromara Village	2	1	Nortel	[8]	

2011/12	Crumlin Star	2	2	Islandmagee	Crumlin Star win 4-3 on penalties[9]

Performance by club

	Team	Wins	Last win
1	Sirocco Works	6	1945/46
2	Drumaness Mills	4	1986/87
=	Nortel	4	1999/2000
4	Albert Foundry (*1923*)	3	1962/63
=	Killyleagh Youth	3	2003/04
=	Larne Technical Old Boys	3	2001/02
7	Abbey Villa	2	2007/08
=	Ards Rangers	2	1979/80
=	Chimney Corner	2	1974/75
=	Comber Rec	2	1957/58
=	Dunmurry Rec.	2	2006/07
=	Islandmagee	2	1998/99
13	Albert Foundry (*1981*)	1	1994/95
=	Ballynahinch United	1	1981/82
=	Coagh United	1	1995/96
=	Crumlin United	1	2000/01
=	Dromara Village	1	2010/11
=	Dunmurry Rec	1	1953/54
=	Grove United	1	2009/10
=	Knockbreda Parish	1	2004/05
=	Newington Y.C.	1	2005/06
=	RUC	1	1964/65
=	Sport & Leisure Swifts	1	2008/09

Sources

- H. Johnstone & G. Hamilton (n.d.) *A Memorable Milestone: 75 Years of the Northern Amateur Football League*
- M. Brodie (ed.) (n.d.) *The Northern Ireland Soccer Yearbook 1999/2000*.
- M. Brodie (ed.) (n.d.) *The Northern Ireland Soccer Yearbook 2000/01*.
- M. Brodie (ed.) (n.d.) *The Northern Ireland Soccer Yearbook 2001/02*.
- M. Brodie (ed.) (n.d.) *The Northern Ireland Soccer Yearbook 2002/03*.
- M. Brodie (ed.) (n.d.) *The Northern Ireland Soccer Yearbook 2003/04*.
- M. Brodie (ed.) (n.d.) *The Northern Ireland Soccer Yearbook 2004/05*.
- M. Brodie (ed.) (n.d.) *The Northern Ireland Soccer Yearbook 2006/07*.
- M. Brodie (ed.) (n.d.) *The Northern Ireland Soccer Yearbook 2007/08*.
- M. Brodie (ed.) (n.d.) *The Northern Ireland Soccer Yearbook 2008/2009*. Belfast:Ulster Tatler Publications

- Newington Youth Club F.C. *Thursday 14th May 2009- Newington are the champions! Newington Football Club* [10]. *Accessed 15-05-09.*
- Northern Amateur Football League [11]

Notes

[1] The original Albert Foundry club folded in 1978.
[2] The current Albert Foundry club was founded in 1981.
[3] Competition not completed after Irish Football Association upheld an appeal against the dismissal of two semi-finalists, but the final was subsequently not played.
[4] Coagh United won the final, but had to return the cup after it was discovered that they had fielded an ineligible player.
[5] "Cup kings Dunmurry are now shooting for a double" (http://www.belfasttelegraph.co.uk/sport/football/local/cup-kings-dunmurry-are-now-shooting-for-a-double-13579255.html). Belfast Telegraph. 2006-12-28. . Retrieved 2012-01-02.
[6] "Sport take cup at their Leisure" (http://www.belfasttelegraph.co.uk/sport/football/local/sport-take-first-cup-at-their-leisure-14122892.html). Belfast Telegraph. 2008-12-30. . Retrieved 2012-01-02.
[7] "Dromara Village 1 Grove United 1" (http://www.belfasttelegraph.co.uk/sport/football/local/dromara-village-1-grove-united-1-14619321.html). Belfast Telegraph. 2010-01-02. . Retrieved 2012-01-02.
[8] "Child's play for Dromara" (http://www.mourneobserver.com/documents/050111SP.pdf). Mourne Observer. 2011-01-05. . Retrieved 2012-01-02.
[9] "Crumlin Star clinch Border Cup after penalty drama at Seaview" (http://belfastmediagroup.com/champions/). North Belfast News. 2012-01-01. . Retrieved 2012-01-02.
[10] http://www.newingtonyc.co.uk/
[11] http://www.thenafl.co.uk/

External links

- The Northern Amateur Football League Official site (http://www.thenafl.co.uk/) - (For fixtures, results and tables of all Northern Ireland amateur football)
- nifootball.co.uk (http://www.nifootball.co.uk/) - (For fixtures, results and tables of all Northern Ireland amateur football leagues)

Inver_Park

Inver Park	
Location	Larne, County Antrim, Northern Ireland
Coordinates	54°50'59.29"N 5°49'34.53"W
Opened	1918
Surface	grass
Capacity	1,100
Tenants	
Larne F.C.	

Inver Park is a football stadium in Larne, County Antrim, Northern Ireland. It is the home ground of Larne F.C.. The land was acquired by Larne in 1918 and has been in continuous use as a stadium ever since. In 2010 the official capacity was set for safety reasons at 1,100 with seating for 656 in the main stand.

In 2010 the club struck an agreement with property developers GML who agreed to build a new stadium on the site that would meet the Irish League's domestic license criteria to enable Larne to play senior football should they win the Championship One in the future in return for Larne's agreement to give up an acre of land adjacent to a development site next to the ground. The deal however has been delayed due to the falling value of the property market, which has led GML to halve their initial bid of £6 million for the land. An agreement is expected in 2011 that will see the project commence by 2012.

References

External links

- IFCP photos from Inver Park (http://home.online.no/~smogols/ifcp/clubs/larne/gallerylarne.htm)
- (http://www.youtube.com/watch?v=yYw7sadHdZw) The Ulster Groundhop video tour of Inver Park

Chimney_Corner_F.C.

Full name	Chimney Corner Football Club
Founded	1952
Ground	Allen Park, Antrim (Capacity: 2000 seats:106)
Manager	Stephen Hughes
League	IFA Championship 2
2010/11	16th

Home colours Away colours

Chimney Corner is an intermediate, Northern Irish football club playing in IFA Championship 2. The club, founded in 1952, hails from Antrim and plays its home matches at Allen Park. Club colours are red and white. The current manager is Stephen Hughes. They have a reserve team which was founded in the 2006–07 season which plays in the Ballymena and Provincial Junior League. They have a large youth set-up which was founded for the 2005–06 season.

The club joined the Northern Amateur Football League in 1953 and became one of its leading clubs before being elevated to the Irish League B Division in 1975. The club stayed at this level until failing to gain a place in the reorganised and re-branded IFA Championship in 2008. The 2008–09 season was spent in the IFA Interim Intermediate League, but the club gained admission to the Championship in 2009, when it was split into two divisions (Corner entering Championship 2).

Current squad

Note: Flags indicate national team as has been defined under FIFA eligibility rules. Players may hold more than one non-FIFA nationality.

No.	Position	Player
	GK	Paddy McKeown
	GK	Andrew Glenn
	DF	Mark Butler
	DF	Darren Marley
	DF	Ryan Gallagher
	DF	Dale Kirkwood
	DF	James McMullan
	DF	Connor Murray

No.	Position	Player
—	MF	Aaron Mitchell
—	MF	Chris Walker
—	MF	Adam Gray
—	MF	Keith Anderson
—	MF	Jackie Todd
—	MF	Mark Tweedie
—	FW	Henry Nutter
—	FW	Corey Agnew

Honours

Intermediate honours

- **Irish League B Division: 2**
  - 1984–85, 1998–99
- **Irish Intermediate Cup: 4**
  - 1967–68, 1981–82, 1982–83, 1996–97
- **Steel & Sons Cup: 4**
  - 1962–63, 1973–74, 1975–76, 1996–97
- **B Division Knock-out Cup: 1**
  - 1986–87
- **Northern Amateur Football League: 5**
  - 1961–62, 1968–69, 1969–70, 1973–74, 1974–75
- **Clarence Cup: 2**
  - 1955–56, 1969–70

References

External links

- Official website (http://www.clubwebsite.co.uk/chimneycornerfc)
- nifootball.co.uk (fixtures, results and tables of all leagues) (http://www.nifootball.co.uk/)

Allen_Park,_Michigan

Allen Park, Michigan	
— City —	
Location in Wayne County and the state of Michigan	
Coordinates: 42°15′17″N 83°12′37″W	
Country	United States
State	Michigan
County	Wayne
Government	
• Type	Council-Manager
• Mayor	William Matakas
• Administrator	David Tamsen
Area	
• Total	7.0 sq mi (18.1 km^2)
• Land	7.0 sq mi (18.1 km^2)
• Water	0.0 sq mi (0.0 km^2)
Elevation	594 ft (181 m)
Population [1]	
• Total	27,616
• Density	4196/sq mi (1617.6/km^2)
Time zone	EST (UTC-5)
• Summer (DST)	EDT (UTC-4)
ZIP code	48101-1952
Area code(s)	313
FIPS code	26-01380[2]
GNIS feature ID	0619983[3]

Allen Park is a city in Wayne County in the U.S. state of Michigan. As of the 2010 census, the population was 28,210. The suburb of Detroit was recognized in Money Magazine's list of America's Best Small Cities.[4] Allen Park is part of the collection of communities known as Downriver

Ford Motor Company is an integral part of the community. Many of the company's offices and facilities lie within the city limits. Since 2002, Allen Park is the practice home of the Detroit Lions and is also the site of the team's headquarters.

Geography

According to the United States Census Bureau, the city has a total area of 7.0 square miles (18 km^2), all land.

History

Allen Park was incorporated as a village in 1927, and as a city in 1957.[5] It was named after Lewis Allen, a well-to-do lawyer and lumberman whose 276½ acres of land (primarily in Ecorse Township) included holdings in what are now Allen Park and Melvindale.[5] Hubert Champaign and Edward Pepper were two other early residents of the area.[5]

In 1950 Allen Park did not include the part of the city directly west of Melvindale, Michigan. This area was still part of Ecorse Township.[6]

Demographics

Historical populations		
Census	Pop.	%±
2000	29376	—
2010	28210	−4.0%

As of the census[2] of 2000, there were 29,376 people, 11,974 households, and 8,202 families residing in the city. The population density was 4,189.7 per square mile (1,618.0/km²). There were 12,254 housing units at an average density of 1,747.7 per square mile (674.9/km²). The racial makeup of the city was 95.6% White, 0.7% African American, 0.36% Native American, 0.81% Asian, 0.02% Pacific Islander, 1.21% from other races, and 1.27% from two or more races. Hispanic or Latino of any race were 4.73% of the population. There were 11,974 households out of which 27.5% had children under the age of 18 living with them, 55.0% were married couples living together, 9.9% had a female householder with no husband present, and 31.5% were non-families. 28.2% of all households were made up of individuals and 14.9% had someone living alone who was 65 years of age or older. The average household size was 2.43 and the average family size was 2.99.

In the city the population was spread out with 22.2% under the age of 18, 6.5% from 18 to 24, 28.2% from 25 to 44, 22.2% from 45 to 64, and 20.9% who were 65 years of age or older. The median age was 41 years. For every 100 females there were 91.0 males. For every 100 females age 18 and over, there were 88.1 males.

The median income for a household in the city was $51,992, and the median income for a family was $63,350. Males had a median income of $50,143 versus $31,168 for females. The per capita income for the city was $24,980. About 1.9% of families and 3.2% of the population were below the poverty line, including 3.3% of those under age 18 and 4.5% of those age 65 or over.

Allen Park's population declined 2.1% to 28,762 by 2003.[1] A 2006 estimate said 27,616 people were living there.[1]

In 2010 the population of Allen Park was 28,210. The racial and ethnic makeup of the population was 87.4% Non-Hispanic white, 2.1% black or African-American, 0.5% Native American, 0.8% Asian, 0.1% Non-Hispanics reporting some other race, 1.6% reporting two or more races, 2.0% Two or more races and 8.1% Hispanic or Latino.[7]

Politics

Former Mayor Gary Burtka resigned unexpectedly on May 31, 2011 due to a recently diagnosed cancer.[8] The former mayor had been under criticism for the failed attempt at securing a movie studio for Allen Park, the purchase of land for the failed studio, and the announcement of a dismantling of the Allen Park Fire Department. As of his departure the APFD has remain unchanged due to overwhelming support from the community.

A new mayor and council were elected in November 2011. Bill Matakas won the race for the top seat. The council members elected were Bob Keenan, Angelo DeGuilo, Dennis Hayes, Harry Sisko, Larry Templin and Tina Gawercki.

Education

Most of Allen Park is within the Allen Park School District. The district has has three elementary schools: Arno, Lindemann, and Bennie. Allen Park Middle School, Allen Park High School, and Allen Park Community School.

Northern Allen Park is within the Melvindale-Northern Allen Park Public Schools. Rogers Early Elementary School is within Allen Park.[9]

World's largest tire

42°16′14″N 83°12′33″W

The Uniroyal Tire in 2006.

Allen Park is home to a roadside attraction, the "Uniroyal Tire", the world's largest sculpture of a tire.[10] Previously a ferris wheel at the 1964 New York World's Fair, the structure was moved to Allen Park in 1966. It is 80 feet (24 m) tall and weighs 12 tons.[10]

World Series of Bowling

In 2009, the Professional Bowlers Association (PBA) announced that Thunderbowl Lanes in Allen Park would be the primary site for the inaugural **PBA World Series of Bowling**. This unique event featured the first seven tournaments of the PBA's 2009-10 season all contested in the same area. One tournament (*Motor City Open*) was contested in nearby Taylor, MI, while the other six (including the *PBA World Championship*) took place at Thunderbowl. The 2009 events ran August 2-September 6, with the televised finals being taped by ESPN on September 5–6.[11]

References

[1] http://quickfacts.census.gov/qfd/states/26/2601380.html
[2] "American FactFinder" (http://factfinder.census.gov). United States Census Bureau. . Retrieved 2008-01-31.
[3] U.S. Geological Survey Geographic Names Information System: Allen Park, Michigan (http://geonames.usgs.gov/pls/gnispublic/f?p=gnispq:3:::NO::P3_FID:0619983)
[4] "Best places to live 2008 - Allen Park, MI" (http://money.cnn.com/magazines/moneymag/bplive/2008/snapshots/PL2601380.html). *CNNMoney Magazine*. . Retrieved 2008-11-24.
[5] Romig, Walter (1986). *Michigan Place Names*. Detroit: Wayne State University Press, p. 18. ISBN 0-8143-1837-1.
[6] 1950 Census. Population Vol. 1. p. 22-32
[7] 2010 population table for Allen Park (http://factfinder2.census.gov/faces/tableservices/jsf/pages/productview.xhtml?pid=DEC_10_PL_QTPL&prodType=table)
[8] "ALLEN PARK: Mayor Gary Burtka resigns, citing health reasons" (http://www.thenewsherald.com/articles/2011/05/24/none/doc4ddc5ba9ab027890535956.txt). *The News Herald*. . Retrieved 2011-05-24.
[9] " Rogers Early Elementary School (http://www.melnap.k12.mi.us/education/school/school.php?sectionid=5&linkid=nav-menu-container-1-3576)." Melvindale-Northern Allen Park Public Schools. Retrieved on November 5, 2011. "5000 Shenandoah *Allen Park, Michigan 48101"
[10] http://www.roadsideamerica.com/story/8258
[11] "FAQs for PBA World Series of Bowling." Article at pba.com/worldseries (http://pba.com/worldseries/FAQ.html#goldenparachute)

External links

- City of Allen Park (http://www.cityofallenpark.org/)
- Allen Park Police Department (http://www.allenparkpolice.org/)
- Allen Park Public Schools (http://www.apps.k12.mi.us/)

Antrim,_County_Antrim

Antrim	
Scots: *Antrìm*,[1] *Anthrim*[2] or *Entrim*[3]	
Irish: *Aontroim*	
 All Saints Church and bridge over the Sixmilewater	
Antrim	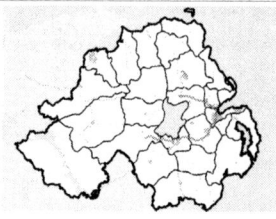 *Antrim shown within Northern Ireland*
Population	Expression error: "20,001" must be numericTemplate:Infobox UK place/trap(2001 Census)
Irish grid reference	J1588 [4]
- Belfast	19 miles (31 km)
District	Antrim Borough
County	County Antrim
Country	Northern Ireland
Sovereign state	United Kingdom
Post town	ANTRIM
Postcode district	BT41
Dialling code	028
Police	Northern Ireland
Fire	Northern Ireland
Ambulance	Northern Ireland
EU Parliament	Northern Ireland
UK Parliament	South Antrim
NI Assembly	South Antrim
Website	[5]

Antrim (from Irish: *Aontroim* meaning "solitary dwelling" [ˈeːnʲtʲrʲɪmʲ]) is a town in County Antrim in the northeast of Northern Ireland, on the banks of the Six Mile Water, half a mile north-east of Lough Neagh. It had a population of 20,001 people in the 2001 Census. The town is the administrative centre of Antrim Borough Council. It is 22 miles (35 km) northwest of Belfast by rail, and was, until recently, also served by the railway line from Lisburn.

History

A battle was fought near Antrim between the English and Irish in the reign of Edward III; and in 1642 a naval engagement took place on Lough Neagh, for Viscount Massereene and Ferrard (who founded Antrim Castle in 1662) had a right to maintain a fighting fleet on the lough.

The Society of United Irishmen launched a rebellion in 1798, which began in Leinster and quickly spread to Ulster. The United Irishmen had been founded in 1791 by liberal Protestants in Belfast. Its goal was to unite Catholics and Protestants and make Ireland an independent republic. Although its membership was mainly Catholic, many of its leaders and members in northeast Ulster were Protestant Presbyterians. On 7 June 1798, about 4000 United Irishmen led by Henry Joy McCracken attacked the town. The rebels were on the verge of taking the town until British reinforcements arrived. Thanks to a rebel band led by James Hope, most of the United Irishmen were able to withdraw safely. This is known as the Battle of Antrim.

Before the Act of Union, Antrim returned two members to parliament by virtue of letters patent granted in 1666 by Charles II.

The Troubles

See also the UDA South East Antrim Brigade

Geography

Divisions and suburbs of Antrim include Ballycraigy, Carnbeg, Caulside, Dublin Road, Greenvale, Greystone, Islandbawn, Meadowlands, Muckamore, Newpark, Niblock, Parkhall, Rathenraw, Riverside, Belmont Heights, Springfarm, Steeple, Stiles, The Folly, Townparks, Massereene.

Climate

As with the rest of the British Isles, Antrim experiences a maritime climate with cool summers and mild winters. The nearest official Met Office weather station for which online records are available is at Aldergrove,[6] under 4 miles to the south of the town centre.

In a typical year the warmest day should reach a temperature of 25.4 °C (77.7 °F)[7] and 2.1 days[8] should attain a temperature of 25.1 °C (77.2 °F) or above in total.

The coldest night of the year averages −6.6 °C (20.1 °F)[9] and 39 nights should register an air frost.[10] The absolute minimum temperature of −14.2 °C (6.4 °F) was reported during the record cold spell of December 2010.[11] In total during that month 10 nights fell to −10 °C (14.0 °F) or below, and the 21st recorded a daytime maximum of just −7.7 °C (18.1 °F).

Demography

Antrim is classified as a large town by the Northern Ireland Statistics and Research Agency (NISRA)[12] (i.e. with population between 18,000 and 75,000). On Census day (29 April 2001) there were 20,001 people living in Antrim. Of these:

- 23.1% were aged under 16 years and 15.7% were aged 60 and over
- 48.6% of the population were male and 51.4% were female
- 32.9% were from a Catholic background and 61.5% were from a Protestant background
- 3.8% of people aged 16–74 were unemployed.

For more details see: Northern Ireland Neighbourhood Information Service[13]

Landmarks

There are many buildings of historic note in the town, especially in and around High Street. The courthouse sits at the end of the street, near the Barbican Gate, the old gateway to Antrim Castle. There are also hidden gems, such as a 19th century smithy (now a shop) on Bridge Street with a distinctive horseshoe entrance.

Antrim round tower

- Shane's Castle and Antrim Castle
- About a mile from the town is one of the most perfect of the round towers of Ireland, 93 feet high and 50 feet in circumference at the base. It stands in the grounds of Steeple, where there is also the "Witches' Stone", a prehistoric monument.
- There was a Castle, near the Six Mile Water, which was destroyed in a fire in 1922. All that remains is an octagonal tower.
- The river allowed the linen industry to be established. The linen industry has been replaced by a Technology Park, the only one in Northern Ireland.
- Antrim Market House is a 2–story building, nine bays long, three deep built in 1726. Formerly a Court House, it is currently being renovated and will house Antrim Information Centre, which is transferring from its existing premises in High Street, and a new multi-purpose auditorium on the first floor providing space for a range of functions including theatre and music promotions.
- The Castle Grounds, that is beside the Antrim Castle.
- The Springfarm Rath

Antrim masonic hall

Transport

Antrim's Aldergrove Airport is the second largest airport in Ireland serving destinations in Britain, Europe and North America. Antrim railway station was opened on 11 April 1848, and closed for goods traffic on 4 January 1965.[14]

Junction One Retail Park

Education

- Antrim Grammar School
- Parkhall College
- Antrim Primary School
- St Comgall's Primary School
- Greystone Primary
- Ballycraigy Primary School
- Parkhall Primary School
- St Joseph's Primary School
- Rathenraw Primary School
- Round Tower Primary School

Sport

- Antrim Hockey Club
- Antrim Rugby Football Club
- Antrim Forum leisure centre[15]
- Chimney Corner F.C.
- Muckamore Cricket Club
- Antrim Mixed Martial Arts Academy[16]
- Ballymena and Antrim Athletics Club[17]
- St Comgall's Gaelic Athletic Club

Notable Antrimers

Antrim was home to author and poet Dr. Alexander Irvine who contrary to popular belief was not born in Pogues Entry in the town but rather in a small house nearby and was raised in Pogues Entry. He later wrote My Lady of the Chimney Corner. This was a reference to his mother. Snooker player Mark Allen who made his crucible debut in 2007 with a first round win over former champion Ken Doherty is from Antrim Town. In 2009 Mark Allen made it to the semi finals of the World Snooker Championships were he lost to eventual winner John Higgins. Maurice Jennings Author of "The Lazarus Legacy" grew up and still lives in Antrim.

See also

- Market Houses in Northern Ireland

References

[1] Ballycopelann Wun-mäll – Department of the Environment (http://www.doeni.gov.uk/niea/ballycopelandwindmillus.pdf)
[2] Languages/Cultural Diversity (http://www.dcalni.gov.uk/index/freedom_of_information/our_policies_and_procedures-2/policies_and_procedures_for_delivering_our_services.htm) Dep. of Culture, Arts and Leisure.
[3] The Ulster-Scot, July 2011 (http://www.ulsterscotsagency.com/ulster-scots-publications/the-ulster-scot/magazine/62/june-2011) Charlie 'Tha Poocher' Rennals.
[4] http://getamap.ordnancesurvey.co.uk/getamap/frames.htm?mapAction=gaz&gazName=g&gazString=J1588
[5] http://www.antrim.gov.uk
[6] "Station Locations" (http://www.metoffice.gov.uk/climate/uk/ni/images/locations.jpg). MetOffice. .
[7] "Annual average warmest day" (http://eca.knmi.nl/utils/calcdetail.php?seasonid=0&periodid=1971-2000&indexid=TXx&stationid=1640). . Retrieved 2011-09-22.
[8] ">25c days" (http://eca.knmi.nl/utils/calcdetail.php?seasonid=0&periodid=1971-2000&indexid=SU&stationid=1640). . Retrieved 2011-09-22.
[9] ">Annual average coldest night" (http://eca.knmi.nl/utils/calcdetail.php?seasonid=0&periodid=1971-2000&indexid=TNn&stationid=1640). . Retrieved 2011-09-22.
[10] ">Average frost incidence" (http://eca.knmi.nl/utils/calcdetail.php?seasonid=0&periodid=1971-2000&indexid=FD&stationid=1640). . Retrieved 2011-09-22.
[11] ">2010 minimum" (http://metofficenews.wordpress.com/2010/12/21/freezing-conditions-continue/). . Retrieved 2011-09-22.
[12] NI Statistics and Research Agency website. (http://www.nisra.gov.uk/)
[13] Northern Ireland Neighbourhood Information website. (http://www.ninis.nisra.gov.uk/)
[14] "Antrim" (http://www.railscot.co.uk/Ireland/Irish_railways.pdf). *Railscot - Irish Railways*. . Retrieved 2007-08-27.
[15] Antrim Forum website. (http://www.antrim.gov.uk/index.cfm?website_Key=27&Category_key=129&Page_Key=487)
[16] Antrim MMA (http://www.antrim-mma.com/)
[17] Ballymena and Antrim A.C Homepage (http://www.baacni.co.uk/)

- This article incorporates text from a publication now in the public domain: Chisholm, Hugh, ed (1911). *Encyclopædia Britannica* (11th ed.). Cambridge University Press.
- Antrim on the *Culture Northern Ireland* website. (http://web.archive.org/web/20080210011323/http://www.culturenorthernireland.org/town_Home.aspx?co=16&to=311&ca=0&sca=0&navID=1)

External links

- Antrim Community Website (http://www.in-antrim.com/)
- Antrim live (http://www.antrimlive.com/)
- Antrim Borough Council (http://www.antrim.gov.uk/)
- Antrim MMA (http://www.antrim-mma.com/)

Association_football_in_Northern_Ireland

Association football in Northern Ireland, widely known as **football** or sometimes as **soccer** (to avoid confusion with Gaelic football), is one of the most popular sports in Northern Ireland. Despite low match attendance at domestic league games, many people have an interest in the English Premier League or the Scottish Premier League.

The governing body in Northern Ireland is the Irish Football Association (IFA) (not to be confused with the Football Association of Ireland (FAI) in the Republic of Ireland).

Governing body

The Irish Football Association is the organising body for football in Northern Ireland, and was historically the governing body for the whole of the Ireland until the FAI split away. The IFA has a permanent seat on the International Football Association Board, which is responsible for the laws of the game.

The **Northern Ireland Women's Football Association** (NIWFA) is the IFA's women's football arm. It runs a Women's Cup, Women's League and the Northern Ireland women's national football team.

Competitions

The domestic league is the IFA Premiership. Some of the major teams include Portadown FC, Glentoran FC and Linfield FC (although Derry City play in the FAI's League of Ireland). A notable historic club was Belfast Celtic, which won nineteen championships before resigning from the league and disbanding after a sectarian riot at its Boxing Day match against Linfield. Derry City FC also left the league following security issues arising from the Troubles, eventually to play in the League or Ireland. In the past some Irish League clubs could draw respectable crowds, on a par with the English and Scottish leagues, but these have fallen heavily over the years.

The Milk Cup is a successful international youth tournament held annually in Northern Ireland, in which clubs and national teams from anywhere in the world may compete. Northern Ireland also played host to the 2005 UEFA Under-19 European Championships.

The Setanta Sports Cup was set up by its sponsors, television channel Setanta Ireland. It is an all-island tournament (two groups of four, then semis and final) featuring eight teams, four being from the League of Ireland and four from the Irish League. Despite fairly low turnouts for each jurisdiction's leagues, the Setanta Cup drew relatively successful gate receipts and in its three-year existence has had one winner from the North (Linfield in 2005).

National team

The Northern Ireland national football team is one of the oldest international teams in the world. It originally played as the Ireland national team until 1950 with players selected from both Northern Ireland and the Republic of Ireland, and competed in the British Home Championship which it won eight times.

The team enjoyed a period of success in the early and mid-80s in which it qualified for two World Cups, most notably in the 1982 tournament in which it topped Group 5 above Spain, Yugoslavia and Honduras to proceed to the second round. After a poor run of form in the late 1990s and first few years of the 21st century, and a corresponding slump in the FIFA World Rankings, there was a subsequent revival in the team's fortunes with home wins over Spain and England. The team came close to qualifying for the 2008 European Championships, and is taking part in a new Nations Cup competition in 2011 along with Wales, Scotland and the Republic of Ireland.

Problems

Sectarian tensions have long been a cause of conflict at football matches in Northern Ireland,[1] and crowd trouble marred games throughout the twentieth century.[2] In 1949, Belfast Celtic withdrew from the Irish League after years of sectarian crowd problems culminated in a Boxing Day match against Linfield at Windsor Park which ended in a pitch invasion and riot in which Belfast Celtic's protestant centre forward, Jimmy Jones, suffered a broken leg.[2]

Since 1968, Cronin argues that the sport has failed to include the Catholic community with Catholic clubs being either forced out of existence or or transferring their allegiance to the FAI.[3] Hooliganism and sectarianism have remained problems throughout the Troubles and up to the present day. Northern Ireland football grounds have been described as "useful sites of public displays of political affiliation", and internal divisions between groups involved in political violence in the mid 1990s was reflected in the supporters of various clubs.[4] Incidents of violence include trouble after Linfield player Conor Hagan was struck by a rocket fired from the crowd,[5] and disturbances between Linfield and Glentoran fans at the 2008 Boxing Day match between the two clubs.[6]

In addition to problems in domestic football, the Northern Ireland international team has also suffered from sectarian problems. In 2002 Celtic player Neil Lennon announced that he would no longer play for Northern Ireland because he received a death threat,[1] and death threats appeared on the walls of loyalist areas including in his home town of Lurgan, Co Armagh.[7]

References

[1] "Sectarianism in sport discussed" (http://news.bbc.co.uk/2/hi/uk_news/northern_ireland/2938575.stm). BBC. 2003-04-11. . Retrieved 2011-03-10.
[2] Richard William Cox; Dave Russell; Wray Vamplew (2002). *Encyclopedia of British football*. Psychology Press. pp. 190, 262.
[3] Mike Cronin (2001), *Catholics and Sport in Northern Ireland: Exclusiveness or Inclusiveness?*
[4] Gary Armstrong; Richard Giulianotti (2001). *Fear and loathing in world football*. p. 53.
[5] "Pictured: The dramatic moment a footballer is hit by a rocket fired by opposition supporters" (http://www.dailymail.co.uk/news/article-1083192/Pictured-The-dramatic-moment-footballer-hit-rocket-fired-opposition-supporters.html). Daily Mail. 2008-11-05. . Retrieved 2011-02-28.
[6] Stuart McKinley (2008-12-26). "Riot police deal with hooligan fans as Linfield beat Glentoran" (http://www.belfasttelegraph.co.uk/news/local-national/riot-police-deal-with-hooligan-fans-as-linfield-beat-glentoran-14121026.html#ixzz1FIcqRfQk). Belfast Telegraph. . Retrieved 2011-02-28.
[7] Colin Blackstock (2002-08-22). "Northern Ireland football captain quits match after death threats" (http://www.guardian.co.uk/uk/2002/aug/22/football.northernireland). The Guardian. . Retrieved 2011-03-10.

See also

- Football in Northern Ireland
- Association football in the Republic of Ireland
- Sport in Ireland

IFA_Premiership

Countries	Northern Ireland
Founded	2008 succeeding Irish Premier League (2003) and Irish Football League (1890)
Divisions	1
Number of teams	12
Levels on pyramid	1
Relegation to	IFA Championship
Domestic cup(s)	Irish Cup Irish League Cup
International cup(s)	Champions League (1 place) UEFA Europa League (2 places)
Current champions	Linfield (2010–11)
Most championships	Linfield (50)
TV partners	Sky Sports,[1] UTV, BBC[2]
Website	http://www.ifapremiership.com/
2011–12	

The **IFA Premiership** – formerly the **Irish Premier League**, and before that the **Irish Football League**–and still known in popular parlance simply as the **Irish League**, is the national football league in Northern Ireland, and was historically the league for the whole of Ireland. Clubs in the league are semi-professional. It should not be confused with the League of Ireland, which is the football league for the Republic of Ireland.

For three seasons from 2009/10 the League will be sponsored by Carling and marketed as the **Carling Premiership**.[3] [4] It is run by the Irish Football Association (IFA). At the end of the season, the champion club is presented with the Gibson Cup – on 26 April 2011 it was awarded to Linfield, the current holders.

The half time and full time scores are carried on the Press Association's vidiprinter service. The full time scores have featured since the start of the 1996/1997 season although the half time scores have only been carried since 2008. The Saturday results are featured in the classified results on Final Score but are not broadcast on Soccer Saturday's classified results service.

History

The Irish League is the second-oldest national league in the world, being formed a week earlier than the Scottish Football League. Only the Football League in England is older.

The Irish Football League was originally formed as the football league for all of Ireland in 1890 (although initially all of its member clubs were in fact based in what would become Northern Ireland). It became the league for Northern Ireland in 1921 after partition, with a separate league and association (the Football Association of the Irish Free State – now called the Football Association of Ireland) – being formed for the Irish Free State (now the Republic of Ireland).

In its first season, seven of the eight teams came from Belfast, and the league – and Irish football – continued to be dominated by Belfast clubs for many years. In 1892, Derry Olympic became the second non-Belfast side, but only lasted for one season. In 1900, Derry Celtic joined the league and, in 1901, a second Derry team, St Columb's Court, was added. St Columb's Court lasted just one season, before being replaced by the league's first Dublin team, Bohemians, in 1903. Another Dublin side, Shelbourne, was added in 1904. In 1911 Glenavon, from the County Armagh town of Lurgan replaced Bohemians, who resigned from the league, but were re-admitted in 1912. During 1912 there were three Dublin sides, with the addition of Tritonville, but, like Derry Olympic and St Columb's Court before them, they lasted just one season. Derry Celtic also dropped out in 1913, so that when the Irish League split in 1921, Glenavon was the only non-Belfast team left.

During the 1920s, however, the league expanded and soon achieved a wide geographic spread across Northern Ireland. Nonetheless, it was not until 1952 that a team from outside Belfast (Glenavon) was crowned champions. Derry City, now of the League of Ireland, played in the Irish League from 1929 until 1972 but eventually resigned during the Troubles after the League voted narrowly to continue a ban on their home ground imposed by the security forces, even after the security forces had lifted it.

From 1995–96 until 2002–03, the League was split into two divisions: the Premier Division and First Division. Since 2003, there has been a single division, albeit with relegation to intermediate leagues below.

In 2003, the Irish Football Association took direct charge of Northern Ireland's national league with the creation of the Irish Premier League (IPL). The Irish Football League retained a separate existence, but controlling only two feeder leagues: the First Division and Second Division. In 2004, the IFA took over control of the remaining IFL divisions and renamed them as the **IFA Intermediate League** First Division and Second Division, effectively winding up the Irish Football League after 114 years.

In 2008, the Irish League was re-organised again (see **2008 Reorganisation** below) and re-named as the Irish Premiership. Teams were invited to apply for membership of the new league, which was reduced to 12 clubs, and places were awarded on the basis of a complicated points system combined with a "domestic licence" scheme.

The League's records from its days in operation as the league for all of Ireland stand as the records for Northern Ireland (as is the case for the Northern Ireland national football team).

Linfield are the current champions, having clinched their record 50th league title on 26 April 2011 after beating sixth placed Lisburn Distillery 4–0 to move 9 points clear with one game remaining.

League format

Each team plays each other three times, making a total of 33 fixtures per team before the "split", when the top six teams play each other for a fourth time to settle the championship and European qualification issues, and the bottom six teams play each other to settle relegation issues. This makes a total of 38 fixtures. After the "split", teams in the top six cannot finish lower than 6th place, and teams in the bottom six cannot finish higher than 7th place, regardless of the results in the final 5 games. The League campaign begins in August and continues until the first Saturday in May. Most fixtures are played on Saturday afternoons, with occasional fixtures on Friday evenings, and some mid-week games, usually on Tuesday or Wednesday evenings. Traditionally, there are Bank Holiday afternoon fixtures on Boxing Day, New Year's Day and Easter Tuesday.

Three points are awarded for a win, and one point for a draw. The team with the most points at the end of the season wins the championship. If two teams finish level on points, goal difference is used to separate them. If teams are still level on goal difference, then the team with the most goals scored is placed highest. Points can be deducted for breaches of rules: for example, fielding an ineligible player.

The League champions qualify to represent Northern Ireland in the following season's Champions League, and the runners-up and third-placed teams qualify for the new Europa League. If the Europa League place that is reserved for the Irish Cup winners (or runners-up, in the event that the Cup winners have also won the League championship) is taken by the team in second or third place, then the fourth-placed team is entered into the Europa League. In order to compete in any of these European competitions, however, clubs must possess a UEFA licence. In the event that a team qualifies without such a licence, lower-placed teams may take their place.

The four highest-placed teams in the Premiership also qualify automatically for the next season's all-Ireland Setanta Cup. The fifth- and sixth-placed teams may also qualify if either or both of the winners (or runners-up, in the event that the Irish Cup winners have also finished first or second) of the Irish Cup and League Cup have qualified via the League. (The League Cup runners-up cannot qualify.)

The bottom-placed team is relegated to the IFA Championship and the second-bottom-placed team must take part in a two-legged play-off match against the second-placed team in the Championship, and is relegated if it loses. (In the event that the Championship winners do not possess a domestic licence, there is no automatic relegation and, instead, the bottom-placed team takes part in the play-off against the second-placed Championship team. In the event that neither the Championship winners nor runners-up has a domestic licence, there is no relegation.)

The twelve Premiership teams also compete for the Irish League Cup: the second-most important cup competition after the Irish Cup.

UEFA coefficient and ranking

As of 13 July 2011, the IFA Premiership's UEFA coefficient points total is 2.583. It is currently ranked by UEFA as the 45th best league in Europe out of 53.

- 43 Albania
- 44 Malta
- 45 **Northern Ireland**
- 46 Wales
- 47 Estonia
  - *Full list* [5]

2008 reorganisation

For the 2008–09 season, the League system for Northern Ireland was re-organised. It was renamed as the **IFA Premiership**, and reduced to twelve teams, included on the basis not only of their performance in the 2007–08 season, but in the previous two seasons, and other off-the-field criteria as follows. Each applicant club was assessed by an independent panel and awarded points against the following criteria:

– *Sporting* (maximum 450 points) – based on league placings, Irish Cup, League Cup and European performances in 2005–06, 2006–07 and 2007–08; with points also awarded for running youth teams, women's teams and community development programmes.

– *Finance* (maximum 200 points) – based on solvency, debt management and cash-flow projection.

– *Infrastructure* (maximum 150 points) – based on stadium capacity, changing provisions, sanitary facilities, field of play, floodlighting, existence and standard of control room, first aid room, drug testing room and media facilities.

– *Business planning* (maximum 50 points)
– *Personnel* (maximum 100 points) – based on qualification and experience of staff
– *Attendances* (maximum 50 points)

Portadown were relegated to the IFA Championship as a result of submitting their application for the IFA Premiership 29 minutes past the deadline for consideration.[6]

Premiership members for 2011–12

Club	Finishing position in 2010–11	First season in top division	First season of current spell in top division	Total seasons in top division
Ballymena United	9th	1928–29	1928–29	73
Carrick Rangers	1st in IFA Championship	1983–84	2011–12	21
Cliftonville	4th	1890–91	1890–91	111
Coleraine	7th	1927–28	1996–97	77
Crusaders	2nd	1949–50	2006–07	62
Donegal Celtic	11th	2006–07	2010–11	4
Dungannon Swifts	8th	2003–04	2003–04	9
Glenavon	10th	1911–12	2005–06	89
Glentoran	3rd	1890–91	1890–91	111
Linfield	**1st**	1890–91	1890–91	111
Lisburn Distillery	6th	1890–91	2002–03	105
Portadown	5th	1924–25	2009–10	80

List of champions and runners-up

Irish Football League

Season	Champions (number of titles)	Runners-up	Third	Leading goalscorer	Goals
1890–91	**Linfield** (1)	Ulster	Distillery	Robert Hill (Linfield)	20
1891–92	**Linfield** (2)	Ulster	Lancashire Fusiliers	Tim Morrison (Linfield)	21
1892–93	**Linfield** (3)	Cliftonville	Distillery	Robert Hill (Linfield) James Percy (Cliftonville)	9
1893–94	Glentoran (1)	Linfield	Cliftonville	Michael McErlean (Linfield)	9
1894–95	**Linfield** (4)	Distillery	Glentoran	George Gaukrodger (Linfield) Joe McAllen (Linfield)	4
1895–96	**Distillery** (1)	Cliftonville	Linfield	*unknown*	
1896–97	Glentoran (2)	Cliftonville	Linfield	Johnny Darling (Linfield) Richard Peden (Linfield)	6
1897–98	**Linfield** (5)	Cliftonville	Glentoran	*unknown*	
1898–99	Distillery (2)	Linfield	Cliftonville	*unknown*	
1899–1900	Belfast Celtic (1)	Linfield	Distillery	*unknown*	

1900–01	Distillery (3)	Glentoran	Belfast Celtic	*unknown*	
1901–02	**Linfield** (6)	Glentoran	Distillery	*unknown*	
1902–03	Distillery (4)	Linfield	Glentoran	*unknown*	
1903–04	**Linfield** (7)	Distillery	Glentoran	*unknown*	
1904–05	Glentoran (3)	Belfast Celtic	Linfield	*unknown*	
1905–06	Cliftonville (1) Distillery (5) (title shared)		Linfield	*unknown*	
1906–07	Linfield (8)	Shelbourne	Distillery	*unknown*	
1907–08	Linfield (9)	Cliftonville	Glentoran	*unknown*	
1908–09	Linfield (10)	Glentoran	Shelbourne	*unknown*	
1909–10	Cliftonville (2)	Belfast Celtic	Linfield	*unknown*	
1910–11	Linfield (11)	Glentoran	Belfast Celtic	*unknown*	
1911–12	Glentoran (4)	Distillery	Belfast Celtic	*unknown*	
1912–13	Glentoran (5)	Distillery	Linfield	*unknown*	
1913–14	Linfield (12)	Glentoran	Belfast Celtic	*unknown*	
1914–15	Belfast Celtic (2)	Glentoran	Linfield	*unknown*	
1915–19	League suspended due to the First World War				
1919–20	Belfast Celtic (3)	Distillery	Glentoran	*unknown*	
1920–21	**Glentoran** (6)	Glenavon	Linfield	*unknown*	
1921–22	***Linfield*** (13)	Glentoran	Distillery	*unknown*	
1922–23	***Linfield*** (14)	Queen's Island	Glentoran	*unknown*	
1923–24	***Queen's Island*** (1)	Distillery	Linfield	*unknown*	
1924–25	Glentoran (7)	Queen's Island	Belfast Celtic	*unknown*	
1925–26	***Belfast Celtic*** (4)	Glentoran	Larne	*unknown*	
1926–27	Belfast Celtic (5)	Queen's Island	Distillery	Joe Bambrick (Glentoran)	28
1927–28	Belfast Celtic (6)	Linfield	Newry Town	*unknown*	
1928–29	Belfast Celtic (7)	Linfield	Glentoran	Joe Bambrick (Linfield)	43
1929–30	***Linfield*** (15)	Glentoran	Coleraine	Joe Bambrick (Linfield)	50
1930–31	Glentoran (8)	Linfield	Belfast Celtic	Fred Roberts (Glentoran)	55
1931–32	Linfield (16)	Derry City	Belfast Celtic	*unknown*	
1932–33	Belfast Celtic (8)	Distillery	Linfield	Joe Bambrick (Linfield)	40
1933–34	***Linfield*** (17)	Belfast Celtic	Glentoran	*unknown*	
1934–35	Linfield (18)	Derry City	Belfast Celtic	*unknown*	
1935–36	Belfast Celtic (9)	Derry City	Linfield	*unknown*	
1936–37	***Belfast Celtic*** (10)	Derry City	Linfield	*unknown*	
1937–38	**Belfast Celtic** (11)	Derry City	Portadown	*unknown*	
1938–39	Belfast Celtic (12)	Ballymena United	Derry City	*unknown*	
1939–40	Belfast Celtic (13)	Portadown	Glentoran	*unknown*	
1940–47	League suspended due to the Second World War				
1947–48	Belfast Celtic (14)	Linfield	Ballymena United	Jimmy Jones (Belfast Celtic)	28

IFA_Premiership

1948–49	Linfield (19)	Belfast Celtic	Glentoran	Billy Simpson (Linfield)	19
1949–50	**Linfield** (20)	Glentoran	Distillery	Sammy Hughes (Glentoran)	23
1950–51	**Glentoran** (9)	Linfield	Glenavon	Sammy Hughes (Glentoran) Walter Allen (Portadown)	23
1951–52	Glenavon (1)	Distillery	Coleraine	Jimmy Jones (Glenavon)	27
1952–53	Glentoran (10)	Linfield	Ballymena United	Sammy Hughes (Glentoran)	28
1953–54	Linfield (21)	Glentoran	Glenavon	Jimmy Jones (Glenavon)	32
1954–55	Linfield (22)	Glenavon	Cliftonville	Fay Coyle (Coleraine)	20
1955–56	Linfield (23)	Glenavon	Bangor	Jimmy Jones (Glenavon)	26
1956–57	**Glenavon** (2)	Linfield	Glentoran	Jimmy Jones (Glenavon)	33
1957–58	Ards (1)	Glenavon	Ballymena United	Jackie Milburn (Linfield)	29
1958–59	Linfield (24)	Glenavon	Glentoran	Jackie Milburn (Linfield)	26
1959–60	Glenavon (3)	Glentoran	Distillery	Jimmy Jones (Glenavon)	29
1960–61	Linfield (25)	Portadown	Ards	Trevor Thompson (Glentoran)	22
1961–62	**Linfield** (26)	Portadown	Ballymena United	Mick Lynch (Ards)	20
1962–63	Distillery (6)	Linfield	Portadown	Joe Meldrum (Distillery)	27
1963–64	Glentoran (11)	Coleraine	Derry City	Trevor Thompson (Linfield)	21
1964–65	Derry City (1)	Coleraine	Crusaders	Kenny Halliday (Coleraine) Dennis Guy (Glenavon)	19
1965–66	Linfield (27)	Derry City	Glentoran	Sammy Pavis (Linfield)	28
1966–67	Glentoran (12)	Linfield	Derry City	Sammy Pavis (Linfield)	25
1967–68	Glentoran (13)	Linfield	Coleraine	Sammy Pavis (Linfield)	30
1968–69	Linfield (28)	Derry City	Coleraine	Danny Hale (Derry City)	21
1969–70	Glentoran (14)	Coleraine	Ards	Des Dickson (Coleraine)	21
1970–71	Linfield (29)	Glentoran	Distillery	Bryan Hamilton (Linfield)	18
1971–72	Glentoran (15)	Portadown	Ards	Peter Watson (Distillery) Des Dickson (Coleraine)	15
1972–73	Crusaders (1)	Ards	Portadown	Des Dickson (Coleraine)	23
1973–74	Coleraine (1)	Portadown	Crusaders	Des Dickson (Coleraine)	24
1974–75	Linfield (30)	Coleraine	Glentoran	Martin Malone (Portadown)	15
1975–76	Crusaders (2)	Glentoran	Coleraine	Des Dickson (Coleraine)	23
1976–77	Glentoran (16)	Glenavon	Linfield	Ronnie McAteer (Crusaders)	20
1977–78	Linfield (31)	Glentoran	Glenavon	Warren Feeney (Glentoran)	17
1978–79	Linfield (32)	Glenavon	Ards	Tommy Armstrong (Ards)	21
1979–80	**Linfield** (33)	Ballymena United	Glentoran	Jimmy Martin (Glentoran)	17
1980–81	Glentoran (17)	Linfield	Ballymena United	Des Dickson (Coleraine) Paul Malone (Ballymena United)	18
1981–82	**Linfield** (34)	Glentoran	Coleraine	Gary Blackledge (Glentoran)	18
1982–83	Linfield (35)	Glentoran	Coleraine	Jim Campbell (Ards)	15
1983–84	Linfield (36)	Glentoran	Cliftonville	Martin McGaughey (Linfield) Trevor Anderson (Linfield)	15
1984–85	Linfield (37)	Coleraine	Glentoran	Martin McGaughey (Linfield)	34
1985–86	Linfield (38)	Coleraine	Ards	Trevor Anderson (Linfield)	14
1986–87	Linfield (39)	Coleraine	Ards	Ray McCoy (Coleraine) Gary Macartney (Glentoran)	14

1987–88	*Glentoran* (18)	Linfield	Coleraine	Martin McGaughey (Linfield)	18
1988–89	Linfield (40)	Glentoran	Coleraine	Stephen Baxter (Linfield)	17
1989–90	Portadown (1)	Glenavon	Glentoran	Martin McGaughey (Linfield)	19
1990–91	*Portadown* (2)	Bangor	Glentoran	Stephen McBride (Glenavon)	22
1991–92	Glentoran (19)	Portadown	Linfield	Harry McCourt (Omagh Town) Stephen McBride (Glenavon)	18
1992–93	Linfield (41)	Crusaders	Bangor	Steve Cowan (Portadown)	23
1993–94	*Linfield* (42)	Portadown	Glenavon	Darren Erskine (Ards) Stephen McBride (Glenavon)	22
1994–95	Crusaders (3)	Glenavon	Portadown	Glenn Ferguson (Glenavon)	27
1995–96	Portadown (3)	Crusaders	Glentoran	Garry Haylock (Portadown)	19
1996–97	Crusaders (4)	Coleraine	Glentoran	Garry Haylock (Portadown)	16
1997–98	Cliftonville (3)	Linfield	Portadown	Vinny Arkins (Portadown)	22
1998–99	Glentoran (20)	Linfield	Crusaders	Vinny Arkins (Portadown)	19
1999–2000	Linfield (43)	Coleraine	Glenavon	Vinny Arkins (Portadown)	29
2000–01	Linfield (44)	Glenavon	Glentoran	Davy Larmour (Linfield)	17
2001–02	Portadown (4)	Glentoran	Linfield	Vinny Arkins (Portadown)	30
2002–03	Glentoran (21)	Portadown	Coleraine	Vinny Arkins (Portadown)	29

Irish Premier League

Season	Champions (number of titles)	Runners-up	Third	Leading goalscorer	Goals
2003–04	Linfield (45)	Portadown	Lisburn Distillery	Glenn Ferguson (Linfield)	25
2004–05	Glentoran (22)	Linfield	Portadown	Chris Morgan (Glentoran)	19
2005–06	**Linfield** (46)	Glentoran	Portadown	Peter Thompson (Linfield)	25
2006–07	**Linfield** (47)	Glentoran	Cliftonville	Gary Hamilton (Glentoran)	27
2007–08	*Linfield* (48)	Glentoran	Cliftonville	Peter Thompson (Linfield)	29

IFA Premiership

Season	Champions (number of titles)	Runners-up	Third	Leading goalscorer	Goals
2008–09	Glentoran (23)	Linfield	Crusaders	Curtis Allen (Lisburn Distillery)	19
2009–10	**Linfield** (49)	Cliftonville	Glentoran	Rory Patterson (Coleraine)	30
2010–11	**Linfield** (50)	Crusaders	Glentoran	Peter Thompson (Linfield)	23

Bold indicates Double winners – i.e. League and Irish Cup winners

Italic indicates Treble Winners – i.e. League, Irish Cup and at least one other senior trophy

Irish Football League First Division

Season	Champions (number of titles)	Runners-up	Third
1995–96	Coleraine (1)	Ballymena United	Omagh Town
1996–97	Ballymena United (1)	Omagh Town	Bangor
1997–98	Newry Town (1)	Bangor	Distillery
1998–99	Distillery (1)	Ards	Bangor
1999–2000	Omagh Town (1)	Ards	Limavady United
2000–01	Ards (1)	Lisburn Distillery	Armagh City
2001–02	Lisburn Distillery (2)	Institute	Dungannon Swifts
2002–03	Dungannon Swifts (1)	Ballymena United	Limavady United

Performance by club

Club	Winners	Runners-up	Winning years
Linfield	50	20	1890–91, 1891–92, 1892–93, 1894–95, 1897–98, 1901–02, 1903–04, 1906–07, 1907–08, 1908–09, 1910–11, 1913–14, 1921–22, 1922–23, 1929–30, 1931–32, 1933–34, 1934–35, 1948–49, 1949–50, 1953–54, 1954–55, 1955–56, 1958–59, 1960–61, 1961–62, 1965–66, 1968–69, 1970–71, 1974–75, 1977–78, 1978–79, 1979–80, 1981–82, 1982–83, 1983–84, 1984–85, 1985–86, 1986–87, 1988–89, 1992–93, 1993–94, 1999–2000, 2000–01, 2003–04, 2005–06, 2006–07, 2007–08, 2009–10, 2010–11
Glentoran	23	23	1893–94, 1896–97, 1904–05, 1911–12, 1912–13, 1920–21, 1924–25, 1930–31, 1950–51, 1952–53, 1963–64, 1966–67, 1967–68, 1969–70, 1971–72, 1976–77, 1980–81, 1987–88, 1991–92, 1998–99, 2002–03, 2004–05, 2008–09
Belfast Celtic	14	4	1899–1900, 1914–15, 1919–20, 1925–26, 1926–27, 1927–28, 1928–29, 1932–33, 1935–36, 1936–37, 1937–38, 1938–39, 1939–40, 1947–48
Lisburn Distillery	6 (inc. 1 shared)	8	1895–96, 1898–99, 1900–01, 1902–03, 1905–06, 1962–63
Portadown	4	9	1989–90, 1990–91, 1995–96, 2001–02
Crusaders	4	3	1972–73, 1975–76, 1994–95, 1996–97
Glenavon	3	10	1951–52, 1956–57, 1959–60
Cliftonville	3 (inc. 1 shared)	5	1905–06, 1909–10, 1997–98
Coleraine	1	9	1973–74
Derry City	1	7	1964–65
Queen's Island	1	3	1923–24
Ards	1	1	1957–58

Total titles won by town or city

Twelve clubs have been champions, and the overwhelming majority have been from Belfast.

Town or city	Number of titles	Clubs
Belfast	100	Linfield (50), Glentoran (23), Belfast Celtic (14), Distillery (6 (1 shared)), Crusaders (4), Cliftonville (3 (1 shared)), Queen's Island (1)
Portadown	4	Portadown (4)
Lurgan	3	Glenavon (3)
Coleraine	1	Coleraine (1)
Derry	1	Derry City (1)
Newtownards	1	Ards (1)

History and trivia

The first Irish League champions were Linfield, and the first runners-up were Ulster. After the first season, the league expanded to ten clubs, but shrank after only one season to six clubs for the 1892–93 season. Only four clubs competed in 1892–93 and 1893–94, then six clubs for the following season, until a membership of eight was achieved for the 1901–02 season. With the exception of one season (1912–13) in which there were ten clubs, membership stayed at eight until the southern clubs resigned in 1920, anticipating the formation of the separate League of Ireland in what would become the Irish Free State. (The League was suspended from 1915 to 1919 because of the First World War.) Only five and six clubs competed in 1920–21 and from 1921–23 respectively, but expansion began with the admission of four new clubs in 1923, another two in 1924 and a further two in 1927, giving a membership of fourteen from 1927 until the League was suspended in 1940 because of the Second World War. When the League resumed in 1947 it was reduced to twelve clubs, and stayed at this number until 1983 when membership was increased to fourteen. In 1990, a further two clubs brought the membership to sixteen, and the League was divided into two divisions (the Premier and First Divisions) of eight in 1995, with promotion and relegation between the two. In 1996 the results from the Premier Division and the First Division started to be featured on the Press Association vidiprinter. In 1997, membership increased again to eighteen, with ten in the Premier Division and eight in the First Division. Between 1999 and 2003, the League had a record twenty clubs in membership. From 1999 to 2002, ten clubs each competed in the Premier and First Divisions and in 2002–03 there were twelve in the Premier Division and eight in the First Division. In 2003, with the creation of the Irish Premier League, the senior league was reduced to a single division of sixteen clubs, although for the first time with relegation to, and promotion from, a league below (a rump Irish Football League in 2003–04 and subsequently the IFA Intermediate League). In 2008, with the creation of the IFA Premiership, the league was reduced to twelve.

Four clubs – Cliftonville, Glentoran, Linfield and Lisburn Distillery – have retained membership of the League since its inception in 1890: 122 years and 111 seasons (due to eleven suspended seasons). All the League members from 1890 up to and including the 2011–12 season (Irish Football League 1890–2003, Irish Premier League 2003–08, IFA Premiership 2008 to present) are as follows (current members shown in bold):

Club	From	No. of seasons	Years
Cliftonville	Belfast	111	1890–
Glentoran	Belfast	111	1890–
Linfield	Belfast	111	1890–
Lisburn Distillery[7]	Lisburn[8]	111	1890–
Glenavon	Lurgan	89	1911–2004, 2005–
Portadown	Portadown	80	1924–2008, 2009–
Coleraine	Coleraine	78	1927–
Ballymena United[9]	Ballymena	77	1928–
Ards	Newtownards[10]	76	1923–2006
Bangor	Bangor	70	1927–2003, 2008–09
Crusaders	Belfast	62	1949–2005, 2006–
Larne	Larne	53	1923–40, 1972–2008
Newry City[11]	Newry	45	1923–40, 1983–2011
Belfast Celtic[12]	Belfast	38	1896–1920, 1924–49
Derry City	Derry	36	1929–72
Carrick Rangers	Carrickfergus	21	1983–2003, 2011–
Omagh Town	Omagh	15	1990–2005
Dungannon Swifts	Dungannon	15	1997–
Ballyclare Comrades	Ballyclare	13	1990–2003
Bohemians	Dublin	13	1902–11, 1912–20
Derry Celtic	Derry	13	1900–13
Shelbourne	Dublin	12	1904–20
Limavady United	Limavady	11	1997–2008
Institute	Drumahoe	10	1999–2006, 2007–10
Queen's Island	Belfast	8	1921–29
Armagh City	Armagh	7	1999–2003, 2005–08
Ulster	Belfast	6	1890–94, 1901–03
Barn	Carrickfergus	5	1923–28
Donegal Celtic	Belfast	4	2006–08, 2010–
Loughgall	Loughgall	3	2004–07
North Staffordshire Regiment	Army team	3	1896–99
Ligoneil	Belfast	2	1891–92, 1893–94
Oldpark	Belfast	2	1890–92
Belfast YMCA	Belfast	1	1891–92
Clarence	Belfast	1	1890–91
Derry Olympic	Derry	1	1892–93
King's Own Scottish Borderers	Army team	1	1903–04

Milford	Milford	1	1890–91
Lancashire Fusiliers	Army team	1	1891–92
Milltown	Belfast	1	1891–92
Royal Scots	Army team	1	1899–00
St Columb's Court	Derry	1	1901–02
Tritonville	Dublin	1	1912–13

Before goal difference was introduced, if the top two teams finished the season with the same number of points, the championship title was decided by a play-off. Nine such championship play-offs took place over the years as follow:

Season	Winners	Score	Runners-up
1895–96	Distillery	2–1	Cliftonville
1898–99	Distillery	2–0	Linfield
1904–05	Glentoran	3–1	Belfast Celtic
1905–06	Cliftonville	0–0	Distillery
Replay	Cliftonville	3–3	Distillery
1910–11	Linfield	3–2	Glentoran
1937–38	Belfast Celtic	2–2	Derry City
Replay	Belfast Celtic	3–1	Derry City
1949–50	Linfield	2–0	Glentoran
1960–61	Linfield	2–0	Portadown
1961–62	Linfield	3–1	Portadown

On one occasion (1905–06), the championship title was shared after Cliftonville and Distillery could not be separated after two play-off matches.

Linfield were the first team to win the championship on goal difference in 1992–93, when they finished level on 66 points each with Crusaders, but eight goals better with a +34 goal difference to Crusaders' +26.

Linfield have won the League championship the most times (50).

From 1890 to 1921, when the Irish League was an all-Ireland competition, no southern clubs (from what would become the Irish Free State and later the Republic of Ireland) ever won the championship. During this period, three southern clubs participated in the League: Bohemians, Shelbourne and Tritonville. The highest place achieved by any of these clubs was second, by Shelbourne in 1906–07.

No club from outside Belfast won the League championship until Glenavon took it to Co. Armagh in 1951–52. In 1957–58, Ards became the first team from Co. Down to win the League, and in 1964–65, Derry City were the first Co. Londonderry team to do so. Of the 111 championships, the title has only been taken out of Belfast on ten occasions. The most successful provincial club is Portadown, with four championships.

A total of 12 different teams have won the championship.

In the early years, Army regiments stationed in Ireland participated in the League: the Lancashire Fusiliers in 1891–92; the North Staffordshire Regiment for three seasons from 1896–99; the Royal Scots in 1899–00 and the King's Own Scottish Borderers in 1903–04.

The longest gap between Irish League championships was 77 seasons (excluding the 11 suspended seasons) between Cliftonville's wins in 1909–10 and 1997–98.

The record for consecutive titles is six, held jointly by Belfast Celtic (1935–40 and 1947–48) and Linfield (1981–87).

Historically, with relatively few league fixtures each season, the Irish League organised a number of other competitions for its members. While some of these enjoyed considerable prestige over the years, they have been phased out over recent seasons due to fixture congestion caused by the expansion of the league and reduced spectator interest. These competitions were: the City Cup; the Gold Cup; the Ulster Cup and the Irish League Floodlit Cup.

In addition, clubs still compete in their respective regional cup competitions: the County Antrim Shield (for clubs within the jurisdiction of the North-East Ulster F.A. (also known as the County Antrim & District F.A.); the Mid-Ulster Cup (for clubs within the jurisdiction of the Mid-Ulster F.A.); and the North West Senior Cup (for clubs within the jurisdiction of the North-Western F.A.).

In 1961–62, Linfield famously achieved the feat of winning seven trophies: the Irish League; Irish Cup; City Cup; Gold Cup; Ulster Cup; County Antrim Shield; and North-South Cup.

On the following occasions, teams have completed a league campaign unbeaten:

Season	Team	Number of games played
1892–93	Linfield	10
1894–95	Linfield	6
1903–04	Linfield	14
1921–22	Linfield	10
1926–27	Belfast Celtic	22
1928–29	Belfast Celtic	26
1980–81	Glentoran	22

The first ever Irish League match to be broadcast live on television took place on 24 September 2007 when Sky Sports showed Cliftonville and Linfield draw 2–2 at Solitude.

Relegation and promotion history

Between 1995/96 and 2002/03, the league was split into two divisions, with promotion and relegation between the two as follows.

Season	Relegated to First Division	Promoted to Premier Division
1995–96	Bangor	Coleraine
1996–97	-	Ballymena United Omagh Town
1997–98	Ards	Newry Town
1998–99	Omagh Town	Distillery
1999–2000	Lisburn Distillery	Omagh Town
2000–01	Ballymena United	Ards
2001–02	-	Lisburn Distillery Institute

At the end of the 2002/03 season, the league was reformed as the single-division Irish Premier League. Four clubs were relegated to intermediate football, and thereafter there has been relegation and promotion between the senior Irish League and the top intermediate league below (now the IFA Championship).

Season	Relegated	Promoted
2002–03	Armagh City Ballyclare Comrades Bangor Carrick Rangers	-
2003–04	Glenavon	Loughgall
2004–05	Crusaders Omagh Town	Armagh City Glenavon
2005–06	Ards Institute	Crusaders Donegal Celtic
2006–07	Loughgall	Institute
2007–08	Armagh City Limavady United Larne Donegal Celtic Portadown	Bangor
2008–09	Bangor	Portadown
2009–10	Institute	Donegal Celtic
2010–11	Newry City	Carrick Rangers

Notes

[1] http://www.irishfa.com/the-ifa/news/3002/northern-ireland-football-lines-up-on-sky-sports/
[2] "Irish League gets TV deal" (http://news.bbc.co.uk/sport1/hi/northern_ireland/2234219.stm). *BBC News*. 2002-09-03. .
[3] Carling to sponsor Premiership (http://news.bbc.co.uk/sport1/hi/football/irish/8161277.stm)
[4] IFA unveils Carling as new Premiership sponsor (http://ifapremiership.com/news210709_1.htm)
[5] http://www.xs4all.nl/~kassiesa/bert/uefa/data/method4/crank2012.html
[6] "Portadown out of Premier League" (http://news.bbc.co.uk/sport1/hi/football/irish/7398872.stm). *BBC News*. 2008-05-13. .
[7] Changed name from Distillery to Lisburn Distillery in 1999.
[8] Moved from Belfast to Ballyskeagh in 1980.
[9] Known as Ballymena until 1934.
[10] Sold home ground in Newtownards in 2002, and subsequently played in Carrickfergus, Belfast and Bangor.
[11] Changed name from Newry Town to Newry City in 2004.
[12] Changed name from Celtic to Belfast Celtic in 1901.

See also

- Northern Ireland football league system
- Irish League XI

References

External links

- Irish Premier League Website (http://www.ifapremiership.com/)
- Irish Football Club Project (http://home.online.no/~smogols/ifcp/UntitledFrameset-15.htm)
- Irish FA Website (http://www.irishfa.com/)
- Irish League Forums (http://www.irishleagueforums.net/)
- BBC Irish Football (http://newsimg.bbc.co.uk/sport1/hi/football/irish/default.stm)

- nifootball.co.uk (http://www.nifootball.co.uk)

Association_football

An attacking player (No. 10) attempts to kick the ball past the opposing team's goalkeeper and between the goalposts to score a goal.

Highest governing body	FIFA
Nickname(s)	Football, soccer, footy/footie, "the beautiful game", "the world game"
First played	Mid-19th century Britain
Characteristics	
Contact	Yes
Team members	11 per side
Mixed gender	Yes, separate competitions
Categorization	Team sport, ball sport
Equipment	Football (or soccer ball)
Venue	Football pitch (or soccer field)
Olympic	1900
Country or region	Worldwide

Association football, more commonly known as **football** or **soccer**, is a sport played between two teams of eleven players with a spherical ball. At the turn of the 21st century, the game was played by over 250 million players in over 200 countries, making it the world's most popular sport.[1][2][3][4] The game is played on a rectangular field of grass or green artificial turf, with a goal in the middle of each of the short ends. The object of the game is to score by driving the ball into the opposing goal.

In general play, the goalkeepers are the only players allowed to touch the ball with their hands or arms, while the field players typically use their feet to kick the ball into position, occasionally using their torso or head to intercept a ball in midair. The team that scores the most goals by the end of the match wins. If the score is tied at the end of the game, either a draw is declared or the game goes into extra time and/or a penalty shootout, depending on the format of the competition. The Laws of the Game were originally codified in England by the Football Association in 1863 and have evolved since then. Association football is governed internationally by FIFA, which organises the FIFA World Cup every four years.[5]

Etymology and names

The rules of football were codified in England by the Football Association in 1863 and the name *association football* was coined to distinguish the game from the other forms of football played at the time, specifically rugby football. The term *soccer* originated in England, first appearing in the 1880s as an Oxford "-er" abbreviation of the word "association".[6]

Within the English-speaking world, association football is usually called *football* (or colloquially *footy*) in the United Kingdom, and *soccer* in Australia, Canada, New Zealand, and the United States. Other countries may use either or both terms, and may also have local names for the sport.

Gameplay

A goalkeeper saving a close-range shot from inside the penalty area

Association football is played in accordance with a set of rules known as the Laws of the Game. The game is played using a spherical ball (of 71 cm (28 in) circumference in FIFA play), known as the *football* (or *soccer ball*). Two teams of eleven players each compete to get the ball into the other team's goal (between the posts and under the bar), thereby scoring a goal. The team that has scored more goals at the end of the game is the winner; if both teams have scored an equal number of goals then the game is a draw. Each team is led by a captain who has only one official responsibility as mandated by the Laws of the Game: to be involved in the coin toss prior to kick-off or penalty kicks.[7]

The primary law is that players other than goalkeepers may not deliberately handle the ball with their hands or arms during play, though they do use their hands during a throw-in restart. Although players usually use their feet to move the ball around, they may use any part of their body (notably, "heading" with the forehead)[8] other than their hands or arms.[9] Within normal play, all players are free to play the ball in any direction and move throughout the pitch, though the ball cannot be received in an offside position.[10]

In typical game play, players attempt to create goal-scoring opportunities through individual control of the ball, such as by dribbling, passing the ball to a team-mate, and by taking shots at the goal, which is guarded by the opposing goalkeeper. Opposing players may try to regain control of the ball by intercepting a pass or through tackling the opponent in possession of the ball; however, physical contact between opponents is restricted. Football is generally a free-flowing game, with play stopping only when the ball has left the field of play or when play is stopped by the referee for an infringement of the rules. After a stoppage, play recommences with a specified restart.[11]

At a professional level, most matches produce only a few goals. For example, the 2005–06 season of the English Premier League produced an average of 2.48 goals per match.[12] The Laws of the Game do not specify any player positions other than goalkeeper,[13] but a number of specialised roles have evolved. Broadly, these include three main categories: strikers, or forwards, whose main task is to score goals; defenders, who specialise in preventing their opponents from scoring; and midfielders, who dispossess the opposition and keep possession of the ball in order to pass it to the forwards on their team. Players in these positions are referred to as outfield players, in order to distinguish them from the goalkeeper. These positions are further subdivided according to the area of the field in which the player spends most time. For example, there are central defenders, and left and right midfielders. The ten outfield players may be arranged in any combination. The number of players in each position determines the style of

A goalkeeper dives to stop the ball from entering his goal

the team's play; more forwards and fewer defenders creates a more aggressive and offensive-minded game, while the reverse creates a slower, more defensive style of play. While players typically spend most of the game in a specific position, there are few restrictions on player movement, and players can switch positions at any time.[14] The layout of a team's players is known as a *formation*. Defining the team's formation and tactics is usually the prerogative of the team's manager.[15]

History

Games revolving around the kicking of a ball have been played in many countries throughout history. According to FIFA, the "very earliest form of the game for which there is scientific evidence was an exercise from a military manual dating back to the second and third centuries BC in China", which was known as *cuju*.[16] The modern rules of association football are based on the mid-19th century efforts to standardise the widely varying forms of football played at the public schools of England. The history of football in England dates back to at least the eighth century.[17]

The Cambridge Rules, first drawn up at Cambridge University in 1848, were particularly influential in the development of subsequent codes, including association football. The Cambridge Rules were written at Trinity College, Cambridge, at a meeting attended by representatives from Eton, Harrow, Rugby, Winchester and Shrewsbury schools. They were not universally adopted. During the 1850s, many clubs unconnected to schools or universities were formed throughout the English-speaking world, to play various forms of football. Some came up with their own distinct codes of rules, most notably the Sheffield Football Club, formed by former public school pupils in 1857,[18] which led to formation of a Sheffield FA in 1867. In 1862, John Charles Thring of Uppingham School also devised an influential set of rules.[19]

England playing Scotland in the first-ever international football game (The Oval, 1872)

The Royal Engineers team who reached the first FA Cup final in 1872

These ongoing efforts contributed to the formation of The Football Association (The FA) in 1863, which first met on the morning of 26 October 1863 at the Freemasons' Tavern in Great Queen Street, London.[20] The only school to be represented on this occasion was Charterhouse. The Freemason's Tavern was the setting for five more meetings between October and December, which eventually produced the first comprehensive set of rules. At the final meeting, the first FA treasurer, the representative from Blackheath, withdrew his club from the FA over the removal of two draft rules at the previous meeting: the first allowed for running with the ball in hand; the second for obstructing such a run by hacking (kicking an opponent in the shins), tripping and holding. Other English rugby football clubs followed this lead and did not join the FA, or subsequently left the FA and instead in 1871 formed the Rugby Football Union. The eleven remaining clubs, under the charge of Ebenezer Cobb Morley, went on to ratify the original thirteen laws of the game.[20] These rules included handling of the ball by "marks" and the lack of a crossbar, rules which made it remarkably similar to Victorian rules football being developed at that time in Australia. The Sheffield FA played by its own rules until the 1870s with the FA absorbing some of its rules until there was little difference between the games.[21]

The laws of the game are currently determined by the International Football Association Board (IFAB).[22] The Board was formed in 1886[23] after a meeting in Manchester of The Football Association, the Scottish Football Association, the Football Association of Wales, and the Irish Football Association. The world's oldest football competition is the FA Cup, which was founded by C. W. Alcock and has been contested by English teams since 1872. The first official international football match took place in 1872 between Scotland and England in Glasgow, again at the instigation of C. W. Alcock. England is home to the world's first football league, which was founded in Birmingham in 1888 by Aston Villa director William McGregor.[24] The original format contained 12 clubs from the Midlands and the North of England. FIFA, the international football body, was formed in Paris in 1904 and declared that they would adhere to Laws of the Game of the Football Association.[25] The growing popularity of the international game led to the admittance of FIFA representatives to the International Football Association Board in 1913. The board currently consists of four representatives from FIFA and one representative from each of the four British associations.[26]

Today, football is played at a professional level all over the world. Millions of people regularly go to football stadiums to follow their favourite teams,[27] while billions more watch the game on television or on the internet.[28] A very large number of people also play football at an amateur level. According to a survey conducted by FIFA published in 2001, over 240 million people from more than 200 countries regularly play football.[29] Football has the highest global television audience in sport.[30]

In many parts of the world football evokes great passions and plays an important role in the life of individual fans, local communities, and even nations. R. Kapuscinski says that people who are polite, modest or even humble in Europe fall easily into rage with playing or watching soccer games.[31] The Côte d'Ivoire national football team helped secure a truce to the nation's civil war in 2006[32] and it helped further reduce tensions between government and rebel forces in 2007 by playing a match in the rebel capital of Bouaké, an occasion that brought both armies together peacefully for the first time.[33] By contrast, football is widely considered to be the final proximate cause in the Football War in June 1969 between El Salvador and Honduras.[34] The sport also exacerbated tensions at the beginning of the Yugoslav wars of the 1990s, when a match between Dinamo Zagreb and Red Star Belgrade degenerated into rioting in March 1990.[35]

Laws

There are 17 laws in the official Laws of the Game. The same laws are designed to apply to all levels of football, although certain modifications for groups such as juniors, seniors, women and people with physical disabilities are permitted. The laws are often framed in broad terms, which allow flexibility in their application depending on the nature of the game. The Laws of the Game are published by FIFA, but are maintained by the International Football Association Board (IFAB), not FIFA itself.[36] In addition to the seventeen laws, numerous IFAB decisions and other directives contribute to the regulation of football. The most complex of the laws is offside. A player in an offside position is only penalised if, at the moment the ball touches or is played by one of his team, he is, in the opinion of the referee, involved in active play, and he is nearer to his opponents' goal line than both the ball and the second-last member of the opposing team. A player is not in an offside position if he is in his own half of the field of play.[10]

Players, equipment, and officials

Each team consists of a maximum of eleven players (excluding substitutes), one of whom must be the goalkeeper. Competition rules may state a minimum number of players required to constitute a team, which is usually seven. Goalkeepers are the only players allowed to play the ball with their hands or arms, provided they do so within the penalty area in front of their own goal. Though there are a variety of positions in which the outfield (non-goalkeeper) players are strategically placed by a coach, these positions are not defined or required by the Laws.[13]

The basic equipment or *kit* players are required to wear includes a shirt, shorts, socks, footwear and adequate shin guards. Headgear is not a required piece of basic equipment, but players today may choose to wear it to protect themselves from head injury. Players are forbidden to wear or use anything that is dangerous to themselves or another player, such as jewellery or watches. The goalkeeper must wear clothing that is easily distinguishable from that worn by the other players and the match officials.[37]

A number of players may be replaced by substitutes during the course of the game. The maximum number of substitutions permitted in most competitive international and domestic league games is three, though the permitted number may vary in other competitions or in friendly matches. Common reasons for a substitution include injury, tiredness, ineffectiveness, a tactical switch, or timewasting at the end of a finely poised game. In standard adult matches, a player who has been substituted may not take further part in a match.[38] IFAB recommends that "that a match should not continue if there are fewer than seven players in either team." Any decision regarding points awarded for abandoned games is left to the individual football associations.[39]

A game is officiated by a referee, who has "full authority to enforce the Laws of the Game in connection with the match to which he has been appointed" (Law 5), and whose decisions are final. The referee is assisted by two assistant referees. In many high-level games there is also a fourth official who assists the referee and may replace another official should the need arise.[40]

Pitch

As the Laws were formulated in England, and were initially administered solely by the four British football associations within IFAB, the standard dimensions of a football pitch were originally expressed in imperial units. The Laws now express dimensions with approximate metric equivalents (followed by traditional units in brackets), though popular use tends to continue to use traditional units in English-speaking countries with a relatively recent history of metrication (or only partial metrication), such as Britain.[41]

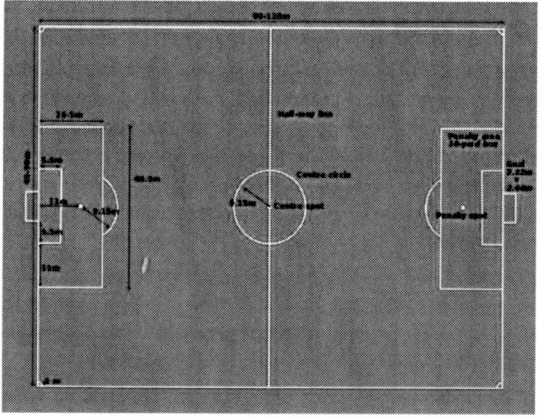

Standard pitch measurements (See Imperial version)

The length of the pitch for international adult matches is in the range of 100–110 m (110–120 yd) and the width is in the range of 64–75 m (70–80 yd). Fields for non-international matches may be 90–120 m (100–130 yd) length and 45–90 m (50–100 yd) in width, provided that the pitch does not become square. Although in 2008, the IFAB initially approved a fixed size of 105 m (344 ft) long and 68 m (223 ft) wide as a standard pitch dimension for A international matches,[42] this decision was later put on hold and was never actually implemented.[43]

The longer boundary lines are *touchlines*, while the shorter boundaries (on which the goals are placed) are *goal lines*. A rectangular goal is positioned at the middle of each goal line.[44] The inner edges of the vertical goal posts must be 7.32 m (8 yd) apart, and the lower edge of the horizontal crossbar supported by the goal posts must be 2.44 m (8 ft) above the ground. Nets are usually placed behind the goal, but are not required by the Laws.[45]

In front of each goal is an area known as the penalty area. This area is marked by the goal line, two lines starting on the goal line 16.5 m (18 yd) from the goalposts and extending 16.5 m (18 yd) into the pitch perpendicular to the goal line, and a line joining them. This area has a number of functions, the most prominent being to mark where the goalkeeper may handle the ball and where a penalty foul by a member of the defending team becomes punishable by a penalty kick. Other markings define the position of the ball or players at kick-offs, goal kicks, penalty kicks and corner kicks.[46]

Duration and tie-breaking methods

A standard adult football match consists of two periods of 45 minutes each, known as halves. Each half runs continuously, meaning that the clock is not stopped when the ball is out of play. There is usually a 15-minute half-time break between halves. The end of the match is known as full-time.[47] The referee is the official timekeeper for the match, and may make an allowance for time lost through substitutions, injured players requiring attention, or other stoppages. This added time is most commonly referred to as *stoppage time* or *injury time*, while *loss time* can also be used as a synonym. The duration of stoppage time is at the sole discretion of the referee. The referee alone signals the end of the match. In matches where a fourth official is appointed, toward the end of the half the referee signals how many minutes of stoppage time he intends to add. The fourth official then informs the players and spectators by holding up a board showing this number. The signalled stoppage time may be further extended by the referee.[47] Added time was introduced because of an incident which happened in 1891 during a match between Stoke and Aston Villa. Trailing 1–0 and with just two minutes remaining, Stoke were awarded a penalty. Villa's goalkeeper kicked the ball out of the ground, and by the time the ball had been recovered, the 90 minutes had elapsed and the game was over.[48] The same law also stands that the duration of either half is extended until the penalty kick to be taken or retaken is completed, thus no game shall end with a penalty to be taken.[49]

In league competitions, games may end in a draw, but in some knockout competitions if a game is tied at the end of regulation time it may go into extra time, which consists of two further 15-minute periods. If the score is still tied after extra time, some competitions allow the use of penalty shootouts (known officially in the Laws of the Game as "kicks from the penalty mark") to determine which team will progress to the next stage of the tournament. Goals scored during extra time periods count toward the final score of the game, but kicks from the penalty mark are only used to decide the team that progresses to the next part of the tournament (with goals scored in a penalty shootout not making up part of the final score).[7]

In competitions using two-legged matches, each team competes at home once, with an aggregate score from the two matches deciding which team progresses. Where aggregates are equal, the away goals rule may be used to determine the winners, in which case the winner is the team that scored the most goals in the leg played away from home. If the result is still equal, kicks from the penalty mark are required.[7]

In the late 1990s and early 2000s, the IFAB experimented with ways of creating a winner without requiring a penalty shootout, which was often seen as an undesirable way to end a match. These involved rules ending a game in extra time early, either when the first goal in extra time was scored (*golden goal*), or if one team held a lead at the end of the first period of extra time (*silver goal*). Golden goal was used at the World Cup in 1998 and 2002. The first World Cup game decided by a golden goal was France's victory over Paraguay in 1998. Germany was the first nation to score a golden goal in a major competition, beating Czech Republic in the final of Euro 1996. Silver goal was used in Euro 2004. Both these experiments have been discontinued by IFAB.[50]

Ball in and out of play

Under the Laws, the two basic states of play during a game are *ball in play* and *ball out of play*. From the beginning of each playing period with a kick-off until the end of the playing period, the ball is in play at all times, except when either the ball leaves the field of play, or play is stopped by the referee. When the ball becomes out of play, play is restarted by one of eight restart methods depending on how it went out of play:

- Kick-off: following a goal by the opposing team, or to begin each period of play.[11]
- Throw-in: when the ball has crossed the touchline; awarded to opposing team to that which last touched the ball.[51]
- Goal kick: when the ball has wholly crossed the goal line without a goal having been scored and having last been touched by a player of the attacking team; awarded to defending team.[52]
- Corner kick: when the ball has wholly crossed the goal line without a goal having been scored and having last been touched by a player of the defending team; awarded to attacking team.[53]

A player takes a free kick, while the opposition form a "wall" to try to deflect the ball

- Indirect free kick: awarded to the opposing team following "non-penal" fouls, certain technical infringements, or when play is stopped to caution or send-off an opponent without a specific foul having occurred. A goal may not be scored directly (without the ball first touching another player) from an indirect free kick.[54]
- Direct free kick: awarded to fouled team following certain listed "penal" fouls.[54] A goal may be scored directly from a direct free kick.
- Penalty kick: awarded to the fouled team following a foul usually punishable by a direct free kick but that has occurred within their opponent's penalty area.[55]
- Dropped-ball: occurs when the referee has stopped play for any other reason, such as a serious injury to a player, interference by an external party, or a ball becoming defective. This restart is uncommon in adult games.[11]

Misconduct

Players are cautioned with a yellow card, and sent off with a red card. These colours were first introduced at the 1970 FIFA World Cup and used consistently since.

A player scores a penalty kick given after an offence is committed inside the penalty area

A foul occurs when a player commits an offence listed in the Laws of the Game while the ball is in play. The offences that constitute a foul are listed in Law 12. Handling the ball deliberately, tripping an opponent, or pushing an opponent, are examples of "penal fouls", punishable by a direct free kick or penalty kick depending on where the offence occurred. Other fouls are punishable by an indirect free kick.[9] The referee may punish a player or substitute's misconduct by a caution (yellow card) or sending-off (red card). A second yellow card at the same game leads to a red card, and therefore to a sending-off. A player given a yellow card is said to have been "booked", the referee writing the player's name in his official notebook. If a player has been sent off, no substitute can be brought on in their place. Misconduct may occur at any time, and while the offences that constitute misconduct are listed, the definitions are broad. In particular, the offence of "unsporting behaviour" may be used to deal with most events that violate the spirit of the game, even if they are not listed as specific offences. A referee can show a yellow or red card to a player, substitute or substituted player. Non-players such as managers and support staff cannot be shown the yellow or red card, but may be expelled from the technical area if they fail to conduct themselves in a responsible manner.[9]

Rather than stopping play, the referee may allow play to continue if doing so will benefit the team against which an offence has been committed. This is known as "playing an advantage".[56] The referee may "call back" play and penalise the original offence if the anticipated advantage does not ensue within "a few seconds". Even if an offence is not penalised due to advantage being played, the offender may still be sanctioned for misconduct at the next stoppage of play.[57]

Governing bodies

The recognised international governing body of football (and associated games, such as futsal and beach soccer) is the Fédération Internationale de Football Association (FIFA). The FIFA headquarters are located in Zurich. Six regional confederations are associated with FIFA; these are:[58]

- Asia: Asian Football Confederation (AFC)
- Africa: Confederation of African Football (CAF)
- Europe: Union of European Football Associations (UEFA)
- North/Central America & Caribbean: Confederation of North, Central American and Caribbean Association Football (CONCACAF)
- Oceania: Oceania Football Confederation (OFC)
- South America: Confederación Sudamericana de Fútbol/Confederação Sul-americana de Futebol (South American Football Confederation; CONMEBOL)

National associations oversee football within individual countries. These are generally synonymous with sovereign states, (for example: the Fédération Camerounaise de Football in Cameroon) but also include a smaller number of associations responsible for sub-national entities or autonomous regions (for example the Scottish Football Association in Scotland). 208 national associations are affiliated both with FIFA and with their respective continental confederations.[58]

While FIFA is responsible for arranging competitions and most rules related to international competition, the actual Laws of the Game are set by the International Football Association Board, where each of the UK Associations has one vote, while FIFA collectively has four votes.[26]

International competitions

The major international competition in football is the World Cup, organised by FIFA. This competition takes place over a four-year period. More than 190 national teams compete in qualifying tournaments within the scope of continental confederations for a place in the finals. The finals tournament, which is held every four years, involves 32 national teams competing over a four-week period.[59] The most recent tournament, the 2010 FIFA World Cup, was held in South Africa from 11 June to 11 July.[60]

A minute's silence before an international match

There has been a football tournament at every Summer Olympic Games since 1900, except at the 1932 games in Los Angeles.[61] Before the inception of the World Cup, the Olympics (especially during the 1920s) had the same status as the World Cup. Originally, the event was for amateurs only,[25] however, since the 1984 Summer Olympics professional players have been permitted, albeit with certain restrictions which prevent countries from fielding their strongest sides. Currently, the Olympic men's tournament is played at Under-23 level. In the past the Olympics have allowed a restricted number of over-age players per team;[62] but that practice ceased in the 2008 Olympics. A women's tournament was added in 1996; in contrast to the men's event, full international sides without age restrictions play the women's Olympic tournament.[63]

After the World Cup, the most important international football competitions are the continental championships, which are organised by each continental confederation and contested between national teams. These are the European Championship (UEFA), the Copa América (CONMEBOL), African Cup of Nations (CAF), the Asian Cup (AFC), the CONCACAF Gold Cup (CONCACAF) and the OFC Nations Cup (OFC). The FIFA Confederations Cup is contested by the winners of all 6 continental championships, the current FIFA World Cup champions and the country which is hosting the Confederations Cup. This is generally regarded as a warm up tournament for the upcoming FIFA World Cup and does not carry the same prestige as the World Cup itself. The most prestigious competitions in club football are the respective continental championships, which are generally contested between national champions, for example the UEFA Champions League in Europe and the Copa Libertadores de América in South America. The winners of each continental competition contest the FIFA Club World Cup.[64]

Domestic competitions

The governing bodies in each country operate league systems in a domestic season, normally comprising several divisions, in which the teams gain points throughout the season depending on results. Teams are placed into tables, placing them in order according to points accrued. Most commonly, each team plays every other team in its league at home and away in each season, in a round-robin tournament. At the end of a season, the top team is declared the champion. The top few teams may be promoted to a higher division, and one or more of the teams finishing at the bottom are relegated to a lower division.[65] The teams finishing at the top of a country's league may be eligible also to play in international club competitions in the following season. The main exceptions to this system occur in some Latin American leagues, which divide football championships into two sections named Apertura and Clausura (Spanish for *Opening* and *Closing*), awarding a champion for each.[66] The majority of countries supplement the league system with one or more "cup" competitions organised on a knock-out basis.

Two players trying to win the ball

Some countries' top divisions feature highly paid star players; in smaller countries and lower divisions, players may be part-timers with a second job, or amateurs. The five top European leagues – the Premier League (England),[67] La Liga (Spain), Serie A (Italy), the Bundesliga (Germany) and Ligue 1 (France) – attract most of the world's best players and each of the leagues has a total wage cost in excess of £600 million/€763 million/$1.185 billion.[68]

Women's association football

Women have been playing association football since the first recorded women's game in 1895 in North London. It has traditionally been associated with charity games and physical exercise, particularly in the United Kingdom.[69] This perception began to change in the 1970s with the breakthrough of organised women's association football. Association football is the most prominent team sport for women in several countries, and one of the few women's team sports with professional leagues.

The growth in women's football has seen major competitions being launched at both national and international level mirroring the male competitions. Women's football faced many struggles throughout its fight for right. It had a "golden age" in the United Kingdom in the early 1920s when crowds reached 50,000 at some matches;[70] this was stopped on 5 December 1921 when England's Football Association voted to ban the game from grounds used by its member clubs. The FA's ban was rescinded in December 1969 with UEFA voting to officially recognise women's football in 1971.[69] The FIFA Women's World Cup was inaugurated in 1991 and has been held every four years since.[71]

See also

- Association football culture
- Association football tactics and skills
- List of association football clubs
- List of women's association football clubs
- List of men's national association football teams
- List of top association football goal scorers
- List of top association football goal scorers by country
- Lists of association football players
- Paralympic association football
- Variants of association football

References

[1] "Overview of Soccer" (http://www.britannica.com/EBchecked/topic/550852/football). Encyclopædia Britannica. . Retrieved 2008-06-04.
[2] Guttman, Allen (1993). "The Diffusion of Sports and the Problem of Cultural Imperialism" (http://books.google.com/books?id=tQY5wxQDn5gC&pg=PA129&lpg=PA129&dq=world's+most+popular+team+sport&source=web&ots=6ns3wVUEGV&sig=SZPKYSDMJBrO1uV4mPxNbKyAuJY#PPA129,M1). In Eric Dunning, Joseph A. Maguire, Robert E. Pearton. *The Sports Process: A Comparative and Developmental Approach*. Champaign: Human Kinetics. p. 129. ISBN 0-88011-624-2. . Retrieved 2008-01-26. "the game is complex enough not to be invented independently by many preliterate cultures and yet simple enough to become the world's most popular team sport"
[3] Dunning, Eric (1999). "The development of soccer as a world game" (http://books.google.com/books?id=X3lX_LVBaToC&pg=PA105&lpg=PA105&dq=world's+most+popular+team+sport&source=web&ots=ehee9Lr9o1&sig=nyvDhcrPoR8lXhYKE7k4CZYg_qU#PPA103,M1). *Sport Matters: Sociological Studies of Sport, Violence and Civilisation*. London: Routledge. p. 103. ISBN 0-415-06413-9. . Retrieved 2008-01-26. "During the twentieth century, soccer emerged as the world's most popular team sport"
[4] Mueller, Frederick; Cantu; Van Camp, Steven (1996). "Team Sports" (http://books.google.com/books?id=XG6AIHLtyaUC&pg=PA57&lpg=PA57&dq=soccer+most+popular+team+sport&source=web&ots=QzydYB5Am0&sig=w_ouIgmegjytYFfWy7k92guTNfU#PPA57,M1). *Catastrophic Injuries in High School and College Sports*. Champaign: Human Kinetics. p. 57. ISBN 0-87322-674-7. . Retrieved 2008-01-26. "Soccer is the most popular sport in the world and is an industry worth over US$400 billion world wide. 80% of this is generated in Europe, though its popularity is growing in the United States. It has been estimated that there were 22 million soccer players in the world in the early 1980s, and that number is increasing. In the United States soccer is now a major sport at both the high school and college levels"
[5] "2002 FIFA World Cup TV Coverage" (http://web.archive.org/web/20061230124633/http://www.fifa.com/en/marketing/newmedia/index/0,3509,10,00.html). FIFA. 2006-12-05. Archived from the original (http://www.fifa.com/en/marketing/newmedia/index/0,3509,10,00.html) on 2006-12-30. . Retrieved 2008-01-06.

[6] Mazumdar, Partha (2006-06-05). "The Yanks are Coming: A U.S. World Cup Preview" (http://www.usembassy.org.uk/rss/transcripts/worldcup2006a.html). Embassy of the United States in London. . Retrieved 2009-06-06.
[7] IFAB. "Procedures to determine the winner of a match or home-and-away" (http://www.fifa.com/mm/document/affederation/generic/81/42/36/lawsofthegame_2010_11_e.pdf) (PDF). *Laws of the Game 2010/2011*. FIFA. pp. 51–52. . Retrieved 2011-03-04.
[8] "How to head a football)" (http://expertfootball.com/training/heading.php). . Retrieved 2011-01-03.
[9] "Laws of the game (Law 12)" (http://web.archive.org/web/20071011115718/http://fifa.com/flash/lotg/football/en/Laws12_02.htm). FIFA. Archived from the original (http://www.fifa.com/flash/lotg/football/en/Laws12_02.htm) on 11 October 2007. . Retrieved 2007-09-24.
[10] IFAB. "Law 11 – Offside" (http://www.fifa.com/mm/document/affederation/generic/81/42/36/lawsofthegame_2010_11_e.pdf) (PDF). *Laws of the Game 2010/2011*. FIFA. p. 31. . Retrieved 2011-03-04.
[11] "Laws of the game (Law 8)" (http://web.archive.org/web/20070913142456/http://fifa.com/flash/lotg/football/en/Laws8_01.htm). FIFA. Archived from the original (http://www.fifa.com/flash/lotg/football/en/Laws8_01.htm) on 2007-09-13. . Retrieved 2007-09-24.
[12] "England Premiership (2005/2006)" (http://www.sportpress.com/stats/en/738_england_premiership_2005_2006/11_league_summary.html). *Sportpress.com*. . Retrieved 2007-06-05.
[13] "Laws of the game (Law 3–Number of Players)" (http://web.archive.org/web/20070913142527/http://fifa.com/flash/lotg/football/en/Laws3_01.htm). FIFA. Archived from the original (http://www.fifa.com/flash/lotg/football/en/Laws3_01.htm) on 2007-09-13. . Retrieved 2007-09-24.
[14] "Positions guide, Who is in a team?" (http://news.bbc.co.uk/sport1/hi/football/rules_and_equipment/4196830.stm). *BBC Sport* (BBC). 2005-09-01. . Retrieved 2007-09-24.
[15] "Formations" (http://news.bbc.co.uk/sport1/hi/football/rules_and_equipment/4197420.stm). *BBC Sport* (BBC). 2005-09-01. . Retrieved 2007-09-24.
[16] "History of Football" (http://www.fifa.com/classicfootball/history/game/historygame1.html). FIFA. . Retrieved 2006-11-20.
[17] "History of Football – Britain, the home of Football" (http://www.fifa.com/classicfootball/history/game/historygame2.html). FIFA. . Retrieved 2006-11-20.
[18] Harvey, Adrian (2005). *Football, the first hundred years*. London: Routledge. p. 126. ISBN 0-415-35018-2.
[19] Winner, David (2005-03-28). "The hands-off approach to a man's game" (http://www.timesonline.co.uk/article/0,,27-1544006,00.html). *The Times* (London). . Retrieved 2007-10-07.
[20] "History of the FA" (http://web.archive.org/web/20050407161619/http://www.thefa.com/TheFA/TheOrganisation/Postings/2004/03/HISTORY_OF_THE_FA.htm). Football Association (FA). Archived from the original (http://www.thefa.com/TheFA/TheOrganisation/Postings/2004/03/HISTORY_OF_THE_FA.htm) on 7 April 2005. . Retrieved 2007-10-09.
[21] Young, Percy M. (1964). *Football in Sheffield*. S. Paul. pp. 28–29.
[22] "IFAB" (http://www.fifa.com/aboutfifa/organisation/ifab/aboutifab.html). FIFA. . Retrieved 2011-12-10.
[23] "The International FA Board" (http://web.archive.org/web/20070422035010/http://access.fifa.com/en/history/history/0,3504,3,00.html). FIFA. Archived from the original (http://access.fifa.com/en/history/history/0,3504,3,00.html) on 2007-04-22. . Retrieved 2007-09-02.
[24] "The History Of The Football League" (http://www.football-league.co.uk/page/History/HistoryDetail/0,,10794~1357277,00.html). Football League. 2010-09-22. . Retrieved 2011-03-04.
[25] "Where it all began" (http://web.archive.org/web/20070608215029/http://access.fifa.com/en/history/history/0,3504,4,00.html). FIFA. Archived from the original (http://access.fifa.com/en/history/history/0,3504,4,00.html) on 2007-06-08. . Retrieved 2007-06-08.
[26] "The IFAB: How it works" (http://www.fifa.com/aboutfifa/organisation/ifab/aboutifab.html). FIFA. . Retrieved 2011-03-04.
[27] Ingle, Sean; Glendenning, Barry (2003-10-09). "Baseball or Football: which sport gets the higher attendance?" (http://football.guardian.co.uk/news/theknowledge/0,9204,1059366,00.html). *The Guardian* (UK). . Retrieved 2006-06-05.
[28] "TV Data" (http://web.archive.org/web/20070922225713/http://fifa.com/aboutfifa/marketingtv/factsfigures/tvdata.html). FIFA. Archived from the original (http://www.fifa.com/aboutfifa/marketingtv/factsfigures/tvdata.html) on 22 September 2007. . Retrieved 2007-09-02.
[29] "FIFA Survey: approximately 250 million footballers worldwide" (http://web.archive.org/web/20060915133001/http://access.fifa.com/infoplus/IP-199_01E_big-count.pdf) (PDF). FIFA. Archived from the original (http://access.fifa.com/infoplus/IP-199_01E_big-count.pdf) on 2006-09-15. . Retrieved 2006-09-15.
[30] "2006 FIFA World Cup broadcast wider, longer and farther than ever before" (http://www.fifa.com/aboutfifa/organisation/marketing/news/newsid=111247/). FIFA. 6 February 2007. . Retrieved 2009-10-11.
[31] Kapuscinski, Ryszard (2007). *The Soccer War*.
[32] Stormer, Neil (2006-06-20). "More than a game" (http://www.commongroundnews.org/article.php?sid=1&id=2079). *Common Ground News Service*. . Retrieved 2010-03-02.
[33] Austin, Merrill (2007-07-10). "Best Feet Forward" (http://www.vanityfair.com/culture/features/2007/07/ivorycoast200707). *Vanity Fair*. . Retrieved 2010-03-02.
[34] Dart, James; Bandini, Paolo (2007-02-21). "Has football ever started a war?" (http://football.guardian.co.uk/theknowledge/story/0,,2017161,00.html). *The Guardian* (London). . Retrieved 2007-09-24.
[35] Drezner, Daniel (2006-06-04). "The Soccer Wars" (http://www.washingtonpost.com/wp-dyn/content/article/2006/06/02/AR2006060201401.html). *The Washington Post*: p. B01. . Retrieved 2008-05-21.

[36] "Laws Of The Game" (http://www.fifa.com/worldfootball/lawsofthegame.html). FIFA. . Retrieved 2007-09-02.
[37] "Laws of the game (Law 4–Players' Equipment)" (http://web.archive.org/web/20070913141601/http://fifa.com/flash/lotg/football/en/Laws4_01.htm). FIFA. Archived from the original (http://www.fifa.com/flash/lotg/football/en/Laws4_01.htm) on 2007-09-13. . Retrieved 2007-09-24.
[38] "Laws of the game (Law 3–Substitution procedure)" (http://web.archive.org/web/20071011144947/http://fifa.com/flash/lotg/football/en/Laws3_02.htm). FIFA. Archived from the original (http://www.fifa.com/flash/lotg/football/en/Laws3_02.htm) on 11 October 2007. . Retrieved 2007-09-24.
[39] IFAB. "Law 3 – The Number of Players" (http://www.fifa.com/mm/document/affederation/generic/81/42/36/lawsofthegame_2010_11_e.pdf) (PDF). *Laws of the Game 2010/2011*. FIFA. p. 62. . Retrieved 2011-03-04.
[40] "Laws of the game (Law 5–The referee)" (http://web.archive.org/web/20070913141909/http://fifa.com/flash/lotg/football/en/Laws5_01.htm). FIFA. Archived from the original (http://www.fifa.com/flash/lotg/football/en/Laws5_01.htm) on 2007-09-13. . Retrieved 2007-09-24.
[41] Summers, Chris (2004-09-02). "Will we ever go completely metric?" (http://news.bbc.co.uk/1/hi/magazine/3934353.stm). *BBC news* (BBC). . Retrieved 2007-10-07.
[42] "Goal-line technology put on ice" (http://www.fifa.com/aboutfifa/organisation/ifab/media/news/newsid=707751/). FIFA. 2008-03-08. . Retrieved 2010-06-19.
[43] "FIFA Amendments to the Laws of the Game, 2008" (http://www.fifa.com/mm/document/affederation/administration/77/82/55/circularno.1145-amendmentstothelawsofthegame-2008.pdf) (PDF). FIFA. . Retrieved 2011-03-04.
[44] "Laws of the game (Law 1.1–The field of play)" (http://web.archive.org/web/20070913142202/http://fifa.com/flash/lotg/football/en/Laws1_01.htm). FIFA. Archived from the original (http://www.fifa.com/flash/lotg/football/en/Laws1_01.htm) on 13 September 2007. . Retrieved 2007-09-24.
[45] "Laws of the game (Law 1.4–The Field of play)" (http://web.archive.org/web/20071011144942/http://fifa.com/flash/lotg/football/en/Laws1_04.htm). FIFA. Archived from the original (http://www.fifa.com/flash/lotg/football/en/Laws1_04.htm) on 11 October 2007. . Retrieved 2007-09-24.
[46] "Laws of the game (Law 1.3–The field of play)" (http://web.archive.org/web/20071011084145/http://fifa.com/flash/lotg/football/en/Laws1_03.htm). FIFA. Archived from the original (http://www.fifa.com/flash/lotg/football/en/Laws1_03.htm) on 11 October 2007. . Retrieved 2007-09-24.
[47] "Laws of the game (Law 7.2–The duration of the match)" (http://web.archive.org/web/20071011144952/http://fifa.com/flash/lotg/football/en/Laws7_02.htm). FIFA. Archived from the original (http://www.fifa.com/flash/lotg/football/en/Laws7_02.htm) on 2007-10-11. . Retrieved 2007-09-24.
[48] The Sunday Times *Illustrated History Of Football* Reed International Books Limited 1996. p.11 ISBN 1-85613-341-9
[49] "Laws of the game (Law 7.3–The duration of the match)" (http://web.archive.org/web/20080603064822/http://www.fifa.com/flash/lotg/football/en/Laws7_03.htm). FIFA. Archived from the original (http://www.fifa.com/flash/lotg/football/en/Laws7_03.htm) on 3 June 2008. . Retrieved 2010-03-03.
[50] Collett, Mike (2004-07-02). "Time running out for silver goal" (http://www.rediff.com/sports/2004/jul/02silver.htm). Reuters. Rediff.com. . Retrieved 2007-10-07.
[51] "Laws of the game (Law 15–The Throw-in)" (http://web.archive.org/web/20070913142556/http://fifa.com/flash/lotg/football/en/Laws15_01.htm). FIFA. Archived from the original (http://www.fifa.com/flash/lotg/football/en/Laws15_01.htm) on 2007-09-13. . Retrieved 2007-10-14.
[52] "Laws of the game (Law 16–The Goal Kick)" (http://web.archive.org/web/20070913141725/http://fifa.com/flash/lotg/football/en/Laws16_01.htm). FIFA. Archived from the original (http://www.fifa.com/flash/lotg/football/en/Laws16_01.htm) on 2007-09-13. . Retrieved 2007-10-14.
[53] "Laws of the game (Law 17–The Corner Kick)" (http://web.archive.org/web/20070913142324/http://fifa.com/flash/lotg/football/en/Laws17_01.htm). FIFA. Archived from the original (http://www.fifa.com/flash/lotg/football/en/Laws17_01.htm) on 2007-09-13. . Retrieved 2007-10-14.
[54] "Laws of the game (Law 13–Free Kicks)" (http://web.archive.org/web/20070913142645/http://fifa.com/flash/lotg/football/en/Laws13_01.htm). FIFA. Archived from the original (http://www.fifa.com/flash/lotg/football/en/Laws13_01.htm) on 2007-09-13. . Retrieved 2007-10-14.
[55] "Laws of the game (Law 14–The Penalty Kick)" (http://web.archive.org/web/20070913142717/http://fifa.com/flash/lotg/football/en/Laws14_01.htm). FIFA. Archived from the original (http://www.fifa.com/flash/lotg/football/en/Laws14_01.htm) on 2007-09-13. . Retrieved 2007-10-14.
[56] "Referee's signals: advantage" (http://news.bbc.co.uk/sport1/hi/football/rules_and_equipment/4188646.stm). *BBC Sport* (BBC). 14 September 2005. . Retrieved 2011-03-04.
[57] IFAB. "Law 5: Referee: Advantage" (http://www.fifa.com/mm/document/affederation/generic/81/42/36/lawsofthegame_2010_11_e.pdf) (PDF). *Laws of the Game 2010/2011*. FIFA. p. 66. . Retrieved 2011-03-04.
[58] "Confederations" (http://www.fifa.com/aboutfifa/organisation/confederations/). FIFA. . Retrieved 2011-03-04.
[59] The number of competing teams has varied over the history of the competition. The most recent changed was in 1998, from 24 to 32.
[60] "The FIFA Calendar" (http://www.fifa.com/aboutfifa/calendar/events.html). FIFA. . Retrieved 2010-06-12.

[61] "Football Equipment and History" (http://www.olympic.org/football-equipment-and-history?tab=1). International Olympic Committee (IOC). . Retrieved 2011-03-04.
[62] "Football – An Olympic Sport since 1900" (http://replay.waybackmachine.org/20090601015157/http://www.olympic.org/uk/sports/programme/index_uk.asp?SportCode=FB). International Olympic Committee (IOC). Archived from the original (http://www.olympic.org/uk/sports/programme/index_uk.asp?SportCode=FB) on 2009-06-01. . Retrieved 2007-10-07.
[63] "Event Guide – Football" (http://olympics.sportinglife.com/olympics/story/0,23911,14986,00.html). *sportinglife*. 365 media group. . Retrieved 2011-03-05.
[64] "Organising Committee strengthens FIFA Club World Cup format" (http://www.fifa.com/tournaments/archive/clubworldcup/japan2007/releases/newsid=570740.html). FIFA. 2007-08-14. . Retrieved 2007-10-07.
[65] Fort, Rodney (September 2000). *Scottish Journal of Political Economy*. **47**. pp. 431–455. doi:10.1111/1467-9485.00172.
[66] "Estudiantes win Argentina Apertura title" (http://msn.foxsports.com/foxsoccer/latinamerica/story/Estudiantes-win-Argentina-Apertura-title). *FoxSports*. Associated Press. 2010-12-13. . "Under the system used in Argentina and most of Latin America, two season titles are awarded each year – the Apertura and Clausura."
[67] Hughes, Ian (2008-03-31). "Premier League conquering Europe" (http://news.bbc.co.uk/sport2/hi/football/europe/7321408.stm). *BBC Sport* (BBC). . Retrieved 2008-05-27.
[68] Taylor, Louise (2008-05-29). "Leading clubs losing out as players and agents cash in" (http://www.guardian.co.uk/football/2008/may/29/premierleague). *The Guardian* (London). . Retrieved 2008-11-28.
[69] Gregory, Patricia (2005-06-03). "How women's football battled for survival" (http://news.bbc.co.uk/sport1/hi/football/women/4607171.stm). *BBC sport* (BBC). . Retrieved 2010-02-19.
[70] Alexander, Shelley (2005-06-03). "Trail-blazers who pioneered women's football" (http://news.bbc.co.uk/sport1/hi/football/women/4603149.stm). *BBC sport* (BBC). . Retrieved 2010-02-19.
[71] "Tournaments: Women's World Cup" (http://www.fifa.com/tournaments/archive/tournament=103/awards/index.html). FIFA. . Retrieved 2011-03-11.

External links

- Federation Internationale de Football Association (FIFA) (http://www.fifa.com/)
- The Current Laws of the Game (LOTG) (http://www.fifa.com/worldfootball/lawsofthegame.html)
- The Rec.Sport.Soccer Statistics Foundation (RSSSF) (http://www.rsssf.com/)

nso:Kgwele ya maoto

rue:Фотбал

Article Sources and Contributors

Sport_&_Leisure_Swifts_F.C. *Source*: http://en.wikipedia.org/w/index.php?title=Sport_%26_Leisure_Swifts_F.C. *Contributors*: A18919, Captainbeecher, Djln, GrahamHardy, Iamstiff, Mabuska, Mooretwin, Wizardman, Прон, 4 anonymous edits

IFA_Championship *Source*: http://en.wikipedia.org/w/index.php?title=IFA_Championship *Contributors*: A. B., Alison, Boothy443, ChrisTheDude, Chrism, DarthJoeyJoJo, Derry Boi, Djln, Edgar81, Ifcp1, John Cardinal, Keith D, Lbr123, MLD, Macunfraidh, Matthew hk, Metropolitan90, Million Little Gods, Mooretwin, Murry1975, MusicInTheHouse, Nonte, Quicksilvre, Reddev87, Sarumio, Siva1979, Skybluekeeper, Tameamseo, Thehelshebang, WereSpielChequers, 33 anonymous edits

Northern_Amateur_Football_League *Source*: http://en.wikipedia.org/w/index.php?title=Northern_Amateur_Football_League *Contributors*: ADL1983, AMuseo, Coccyx Bloccyx, DarthJoeyJoJo, Djln, Jmorrison230582, Luk, Lyrl, MTC, Mooretwin, Number 57, RHaworth, Ryannus, Sarumio, Stb74, Thrlrds2007, Weejack48, 15 anonymous edits

Inver_Park *Source*: http://en.wikipedia.org/w/index.php?title=Inver_Park *Contributors*: Alai, ArchStanton69, Ardfern, BrownHairedGirl, Captainbeecher, Djln, Ifcp1, Jonathan Winsky, Kafuffle, Mellery, Mooretwin, Mr Sheep Measham, Patken4, ProffesorX, Severo, Ted Ted, Willy turner, 2 anonymous edits

Chimney_Corner_F.C. *Source*: http://en.wikipedia.org/w/index.php?title=Chimney_Corner_F.C. *Contributors*: 21655, A18919, Aecis, Ardfern, Boothy443, Daff4555, DarthJoeyJoJo, Djln, Dribblingscribe, Favonian, Grayshi, Iamstiff, Ifcp1, Irregulargalaxies, Jogurney, Lcawte, Mabuska, Million Little Gods, Mooretwin, Princeprospero, Reddev87, Sarumio, Sjorford, Stb74, Stevef82, Steven Zhang, Thrlrds2007, UnqstnableTruth, WikHead, Wizardman, 47 anonymous edits

Allen_Park,_Michigan *Source*: http://en.wikipedia.org/w/index.php?title=Allen_Park%2C_Michigan *Contributors*: A2Kafir, Acntx, Alansohn, Apdramaqueen13, Banaticus, Betacommand, Bkonrad, Blackthunder326, Bobby H. Heffley, Burntsauce, Caiaffa, Colchester121891, Criticalthinker, Eco84, Feezo, Funnyhat, Giraffedata, GrahamHardy, Howenstein115, Infosponge1995, Insertnamehere, Isotope23, Ixfd64, Jasonn, Jay Timko, Jaytiger, Jguad1, Jim2029, Jllm06, John254, Johnpacklambert, Joncaire, KrakatoaKatie, L Kensington, Leonard^Bloom, Lightmouse, Linksfuss, MONGO, Mapsax, Mbr7975, Mike Christie, Mirage5000, Monegasque, Mreddy1, Nick Number, Oxymoron83, PhilKnight, Postdlf, QueenCake, Ram-Man, Rawling, Reboot3333, Recognizance, ReyBrujo, Rhettfox, Rich Farmbrough, RxS, ScargO212, Seth Ilys, Sfoskett, Shereth, Slyguy, Steven.williams32333, The wub, Thomas Paine1776, Tide rolls, Troyoda1990, Unforgiven24, Vsmith, Wayne Slam, WhisperToMe, Wikih101, X96lee15, ZooFari, 156 anonymous edits

Antrim,_County_Antrim *Source*: http://en.wikipedia.org/w/index.php?title=Antrim%2C_County_Antrim *Contributors*: Anaxial, Angr, Ardfern, Asarlaí , Bangee, Biggiewiggler, Biruitorul, Blowdart, Boothy443, Canterbury Tail, Census1911 fan, Clarkekentyboy, Cmconraoi, Cmr08, Cnyborg, CryptoDerk, Damnbutter, Darklilac, Denzell393, Dgri, Discospinster, EJF, Factocop, Fences and windows, Frankie816, Fyyer, Gallagher-Glass, Giggleboos, Gilliam, Haltiamieli, Harry knight, J.delanoy, JaGa, Jguk, Jimbetruth, Jimgawn, JonHarder, Jonchapple, Jvlm.123, Jza84, Kbdank71, Keith D, Keys767, Lozleader, MER-C, MJ94, Mabuska, Man vyi, Masti, Matt Deres, Million Little Gods, Misskg, Mma superstar, Mooretwin, Morwen, NOidentity, Nicohn, NotMuchToSay, O Fenian, Operato, Orioane, Peter Clarke, Peter.C, PrincessofLlyr, Pwqn, Qed2u, Rich Farmbrough, Rjwilmsi, Ro2000, SFC9394, SJFriedl, SalopianJames, Setanta747 (locked), SheeEttin, SunCreator, TAL81, Tassedethe, Tuspm, Unknownserv, WRK, Weesteekyaja, Whydontyoucallme dantheman, Ww2censor, Xsheriffx, Xxxeditxxx, Zoney, Zotel, 138 anonymous edits

Association_football_in_Northern_Ireland *Source*: http://en.wikipedia.org/w/index.php?title=Association_football_in_Northern_Ireland *Contributors*: A18919, CambridgeBayWeather, Darryl.matheson, Djln, Eamonnca1, Gnevin, GordyB, HighKing, Hugo999, Jza84, Kevin McE, Kotniski, Lightmouse, Lord Cornwallis, Mintymoonbeams, Mooretwin, Mxshee, Robofish, Smsarmad, Stb74, Tabletop, Tameamseo, Thumperward, Tomwhittaker27, 15 anonymous edits

IFA_Premiership *Source*: http://en.wikipedia.org/w/index.php?title=IFA_Premiership *Contributors*: A. B., Alejoruiz mayo, Andygray110, Astrotrain, BRACK66, Betacommand, BigDunc, Bjmullan, Bkonrad, Blue Elf, Boothy443, Chrism, Commander Shepard, D.brodale, Dale Arnett, Darryl.matheson, Darth rumsfeld, Darwinek, Derry Boi, Distilleryfan, Djln, Ealusmith, Everton, Fasach Nua, Flowerpotman, Football247365, Fribbler, Gazza63, Gonger1321, Harryboyles, High Flying Dwarf, HonorTheKing, Ief, Ifcp1, Ionutzmovie, Iridescent, JHunterJ, Jahiegel, Jmcnally, Jmorrison230582, John Cardinal, KaragouniS, Koavf, Koppapa, Lexusuns, Lyrl, MTC, Maccabi Netanya Rules, Macphisto, Marianocecowski, Matthew hk, Maxim, Mayumashu, Mooretwin, Mr Parker, Mtndrums, Murry1975, MusicInTheHouse, Nameless User, Nick Number, Nishisuke1983, O Fenian, Onetonycousins, Philipb78, Prosperosmask, Quadell, RedRazor, Reddev87, Rettetast, Rjwilmsi, Rst20xx, Saint9016, Salt Yeung, Simianvector, SirFozzie, Soccer-holic, Stb74, Stone roller, Stutelad, SunnyDSunnyD, Tangerines, The C of E, TheBigJagielka, Thehelshebang, Thumperward, Zzuuzz, 169 anonymous edits

Association_football *Source*: http://en.wikipedia.org/w/index.php?title=Association_football *Contributors*: 'Arry Boy, 03BTHOMPSON, 05fcrane, 10metreh, 1337B3A57, 144.132.75.xxx, 194.109.232.xxx, 1burke, 1crywolf1, 200120037, 209.20.225.xxx, 21655, 24.218.142.xxx, 24fan24, 2writer, 4019jimmyw, 540dash, 62.253.64.xxx, 62.7.47.xxx, 62.7.5.xxx, 63.192.137.xxx, 84user, A-giau, A.a679100, AEMoreira042281, ARrohetMeZemer, Aabha R, Aaron1716, Abc123youwantme, Aberdeen fc, Abigail-II, Abrech, Abu badali, Academic Challenger, Acalamari, Accurizer, Achinn, AdamWeeden, Adambro, Addshore, Adizlaja, Admrboltz, AdrianTM, Adzeds, Aeon1006, Aeons, Aesopos, Aftesk, Agentknight, AgnosticPreachersKid, Aheyfromhome, Ahills60, Ahoerstemeier, AileanMacRaith, Airconswitch, AirdishStraus, Aitias, Aj hicks, Ajaxkroon, Akamad, AkdenizliAslan, Aksi great, Aladdinlee, Albinomonkey, Ale jrb, AlefZet, Aleksandr Grigoryev, Alex.muller, Alex43223, Alexis, Alexisamattlover, Alexsh, Alexsoccer102, Alexwiki69, Algebra, Alias Flood, Alsandro, Amalthea, Amazonien, Ambrose222, Ambuj.Saxena, AmiDaniel, AmishThrasher, Amitch, Amorymeltzer, Ams80, AnOddName, AnakngAraw, Anand Bindra, Anaraug, AndeanThunder, Anders Torlind, Anders Törlind, Andocomando, Andonic, Andreasegde, Andres, Andrew Levine, Andrewlp1991, Andries, Andrij Kursetsky, Andrwsc, Andy Marchbanks, Angelo.romano, Angles theatre, Angmering, Angus Lepper, Angusmclellan, Anish9807, Anonywiki, Antandrus, Anthony, Anthonyd3ca, Anyabean17, Aplomado, Aranherunar, Arbor, AriGold, Arnemann, Art LaPella, Arthena, Arthur Holland, Arwel Parry, Asdackla, Ashesdhakal, AshleyMorton, Asmah01, AstroNomer, Astrovega, Atari 667, Athaenara, Atharshiraz, Athomas7990, Attilios, Aubtiger2008, Aude, Auntof6, Australian Matt, Autoerrant, AutomaticWriting, Autonova, Auxil, Avitaltr, Avs5221, Awesome511, AxelBoldt, Aymatth2, Az1568, Azzurro2882, B.Wind, B4hand, BACthegreat, BBJAPS3, BGTopDon, BKH2007, BRG, BUblogger, Babylon32, Baconfish, Badgernet, Bagpuss, Baldhur, Ballboys10, Balthazarduju, Balwan, Bananaman69, Bangaluru, Banhtrung1, Barcafan10, Baristarim, Barliner, BarretB, Bart133, Basawala, Basbll4lif23, Baseballbrett13, Bastin, Batman2005, BatteryIncluded, Bawolff, Bbatsell, Bearbug21, Beeman20, Behzad20, Ben davison, Ben-Zin, Ben9dan16, Bender235, Bennelliott, Bennybp, Bento00, Betelgeuse, Beve, Bevo, Bevo74, Bgates456, Bhrdkor123, Biatch, BierHerr, Big Jock Knew, Bigdumbredman2, Bigearedtiger, Bigeazy, Biggieyankfan, Bigpapawaka, Bikeable, BillWSmithJr, Billward, Bkitko, Bkonrad, Blarg000001, Bleakcomb, Bletch, Blokee, Blotsfan, Blue520, Bluelion, Boavi, Bob Palin, Bob schriver, Bob199393, Bob512012, Bobaldinho10, Bobblewik, Bobo192, Bobomg, Bobryuu, Bogdangiusca, Boing! said Zebedee, Bomchickawah, Bongwarrior, Boojanam01, Boole, Borisblue, Bornfury, Bornintheguz, Boshtang, Boychoir, Bozzzzz, Brad101, Branddobbe, Brandeis, Branko, BreenJnr2@aol.com, Breezeonhold, Brendanurbanwarrior, Brent william mccoy, Brentonf, Brian0918, Brickie, Brighterorange, Brion VIBBER, Brisngr, BritishWatcher, Brod7, Brossow, Bruce1ee, Bryan Derksen, Bryansprang, Bssc81, Btljs, Bubba hotep, Bubbla, Buchanan-Hermit, Bullzeye, Bunnyho1, Bwithh, Byrdman15, ByteofKnowledge, Bz2, C.Fred, C12H22O11, CJ, CPMcE, CS.Aussie, CWii, Cactus.man, Cafzal, Caharayo, CahirAndIrish, Calsicol, Caltas, CambridgeBayWeather, Cameron5dollars, Camerong, Can't sleep, clown will eat me, CanbekEsen, Canek, Canjth, Captain-n00dle, Card Football King, Cardsplayer4life, Carnun, Carreira, Casablanca2000in, Casey56, Casper2k3, Castlecraver, Cataphract, Catch47, CatsClaw, Cbrown1023, Cdc, Cedders, Centrx, Ceoil, Cfarzan, Cfcrowdies18, Cfrydj, Chabby, Chalkwalker, Chandler, Chanheigeorge, CharlieZeb, CharlotteWebb, ChaucerGeoffrey, Checkmate911, Chibinho, Chill doubt, Chillum, Chinesekage, Chingiss, Chkno, Chodorkovskiy, Chris Roy, ChrisTheDude, Chrishatch1973, Chrislk02, Chrism, Christpunkergirl, Chrmb, Chromancer, Chuq, Citizen Premier, Ckatz, Clamster5, Clawed, Clio64B, Clngre, Clocksarecool, Clout, Cls14, ClubOranje, Clydecoast, Cmdrjameson, Cncxbox, Cobaltbluetony, Cobaltcigs, Cocoaguy, Code E, Code phil, Codex Sinaiticus, Cold Season, Colin stuart, Colin9brown, Colipon, Collard, Colonies Chris, Commander Shepard, CommonsDelinker, ComputerGuy, Conscious, Conversion script, Cookiva, Coolcaesar, Corean2006, Corvus cornix, Costlab, Counsell, Courtney03, Crafedog, Craig Staples, Craigman0101, Craitman17, Crazycomputers, Crazytales, CreerBFC, Cribananda, Crissov, Cristian Cappiello, Crosstimer, Crystallina, Cs-wolves, CtrlAltDek, Cuchullain, Cuecho, Curps, Custodio.oliveira, Cutler, Cuvette, Cyan, Cybercobra, Cybershore, Cyp, DANE RAMADAN YOUSSEF, DARTH SIDIOUS 2, DB, DGJM, DIEXEL, DJ Clayworth, DOwenWilliams, DVD R W, Da Mastaa, DaGizza, Dachamp724, Dacxjo, Daddy Kindsoul, Daduzi, Daemonic Kangaroo, Daftpunkboy93, Dahliarose, Dale Arnett, Damienhunter, Dan Atkinson, Dan the man 10, DanKeshet, DanRUK, DancingPenguin, Daniel, Daniel Case, Daniel.Cardenas, Daniel5127, Daniel987600, Danlina, Danltn, Danreitz, Dantedanger, Dantheman0056, Dantheman531, Danthemankhan, Daquios, Darkildor, Darkrifle, Darry2385, Darthgriz98, Dave.Dunford, Dave101, Daveb, Davewild, David Johnson, David Levy, David Schaich, Davidbrookesland, Dc19, Ddfree, Deadlock, Deadmanwalking1, Deanh, Debate987, Deeb, Delirium, Delldot, Deltabeignet, Den fjättrade ankan, Dendodge, Denhamd2, DerHexer, Derek Ross, Derild4921, Deus Ex, Didier13, DiegoTristan, Differentgravy, Digitalme, Dijon312, Dim SIM.StPaTs, Dimitrakopulos, Dina, Dinis80654, Dinshoupang, Dirkbb, DirkvdM, Disavian, Discospinster, Disorganized 676, Diving2010, Djdan90, Djln, Djmadd93, Doc glasgow, DocWatson42, Docu, Document, Doglover77, Dojarca, Domcabcd, Donama, Donatj, Donfbreed, Dostal, Doubleslash, Downloadmeh, Dr Santa, Dr31, DrKiernan, Dradious, DragonHawk, DragonflySixtyseven, Dragonnas, Draicone, Drmies, Dryazan, Dudesleeper, Duja, Durin, Dust Filter, Dustimagic, Dweller, Dycedarg, DylaHeary, DylanW, EBL, EEMIV, EJF, EPs, ERcheck, ESkog, EWS23, Eagle4000, Earl CG, East718, Ebeisher, Eceresa, Eclecticology, Ed Poor, Ed g2s, EdC, Eddyji999, Edgar181, Eielsonafbman, Einstein100, El Suizo, Elliskev, Emc2, Empty Buffer, Emura, Encephalon, Endroit, Endymi0n, Energyfreezer, Enigmaman, Enoch Wong, Enviroboy, Epsteada, Equazcion, Erath, Ergmuncer, Ericoides, Error, Erzengel, Esanchez7587, Esperant, Estel, Eu.stefan, Evekrogman, Evenmadderjon, Evercat, Everyking, Evice, Evillution, Ewen, Executive.koala, Exploding Boy, Ezeu, Ezhiki, FF2010, Fabian9, Facts707, Fadf, FaerieInGrey, Fainites, Falcon8765, Fan-1967, Fang Aili, Fanta206, Fastily, Fasttimes68, Father Goose, Favonian, FelisLeo, Felix Portier, Fernandopascullo, Feroang, Fewskulchor, Ffahm, Finell, First Light, FisherQueen, Fleagle11, Fliffy, FlipCockle, Floodamanny, Floridan, Fluffernutter, FluffyWhiteCat, Fluke08, Fmhsxc2010, Fonsildiamond, Fonzy, Football Fan Zone, Footballhead, Footeditor, ForeverWhiteRose, Forshizzle, Foxlarocks, Fr. Jim, Fragbase, Fraggle81, FrancoGG, Frank87, FrankCostanza, Freakofnurture, Fredrik, Freepenguin, FreplySpang, Frischy, Froogoleer, Fruit666, Frymaster, Funandtrvl, Funknl, Funnyfumble5, Fuzzle, Fvasconcellos, Fvw, Fyyer, G-Man, GHoeberX, GVnayR, Gar, Gareth Owen, Garzo, Gaulwiki, Gavinho, Gaw jess, Gazcheung, Gciriani, Gdarin, Gdo01, Gene Nygaard, Geoff janes, Geopersona, George The Dragon, Georgia guy, Gergerballball, German Player, Gerrit, Ghosts&empties, GianniG46, GiantSnowman, Giants2008, Giff1002, Gilesz182, Gilliam, Gilmore Guy, Gilo1969, Gimboid13, Ginajanota, Girlslutgirl, Gizmoleeds, Gkhoyt, Glass Sword, Glen, Globalsolidarity, Gman124, Gnangarra, Gnevin, Goatherd, Godneck, Gogo Dodo, Gohoos13, Gohoos131, Goldfinger820, Gollumz001,

Article Sources and Contributors 64

Gooface, Gordongeiger, Grabbies200, Grace Note, GraemeL, GraemeLeggett, Grafen, Graham87, Grant.Alpaugh, Grant65, Green, Greenman, Gregoryj83, Grey Shadow, Gridlock Joe, Griffinofwales, Grm wnr, Grondemar, GroveWanderer, Grover cleveland, Grunners, Gun Powder Ma, Gunray, Gurch, Gwcstcs, Gwernol, Gytrem, Gz33, Hadal, Hadger, Hagerman, Hairchrm, Hairouna, Hairy Dude, Hajima, Haldraper, HalfShadow, Halogeek, HandsomeFella, Happy2, HappyCamper, Happysailor, Harry Hotspur, Harry Potter, Harry19023, Hashimjaved, Haukurth, Hawkeye7, Hayden5650, Hegemon7786, Heightwatcher, Hemanshu, Henrygb, Hephaestos, Herbert Shek, Herbertxu, Heron, Hesamj, Hesperian, Hflegit16, Hgrenbor, Hi little kids, Hig Hertenfleurst, HighKing, His Ryanness, Hmains, Hockeyplayer371, Hollandfan, Holyjoe, Homer slips., Homestarmy, HomieG2008, Honette, HonorTheKing, Horologium, Htews, HungrySphynx2241, Husky, Husond, I already forgot, IJK Principle, INkubusse, Iahead, Iamajpeg, Iamthecutestboyever, Iangibbins, Ichinisan Ilu, Igiffin, Igor, Ihatenyy13, ImperatorExercitus, Imroy, Inhumandecency, Innotata, Intelati, Intellectualfive, Inter16, Interchange88, Iohjasdb, Ionutzmovie, Iota, Iran11, IronGargoyle, Isadera, Isfalk, Itsmine, IvoJovo, Ixfd64, Izelpii, Izno, J Di, J Hofmann Kemp, J.delanoy, JCam, JDDJS, JForget, JFreeman, JHMM13, JIP, JJGD, JLINCON, JNW, JRHorse, JSpudeman, JStewart, JYolkowski, Jacek Kendysz, Jack forbes (renamed), JackieMa, Jackosta1234, Jacoplane, Jacquerie27, Jaffer, Jahiegel, Jake2392, James Foulds, James530, JamesBWatson, JamesMLane, Jamesr@thesportbar.com, Jandrews23jandrews23, Jaranda, Jason Potter, Java13690, Jaxl, Jchild, Jcrow43, Jdawg4820, Jed, Jeff.nolan, Jeff3000, Jennie--x, Jenny4life, JeongHW, JeremyA, Jeronimo, Jersyko, Jesismael, Jesus182, Jfg284, Jhenderson777, Jibbajabba, Jiggelmaster7, Jimfbleak, Jimgawn, Jklin, Jmcc150, Jmed123, Jnestorius, Jni, JoanneB, Joe Cannon Fan, JoeLatics, Joebamber1990, Joebloggsy, Johan Dahlin, Johan Elisson, John, John Anderson, John Reid, JohnOwens, Johnmc, Johnny Jane, Johnnyonthespot, JonBroxton, JonC, JonHarder, Jonik, Jonnysamleland, Jooler, Jor70, Jose77, Joseph Solis in Australia, Joseph Wajsberg, Josh167, Josh619112345267, JoshDuffMan, Josquius, Jossi, Journalist, Joy, Joyous!, Jpogi, Jpollar, Jrdragster11, Jrodes, Jtdirl, Jtkiefer, Jtle515, Ju66l3r, Juancamaney22, Jujutacular, Julia Brewer, Julianp, JuneGloom07, Jusdafax, Jwissick, KIPKIP, Kabillion, Kablammo, Kafziel, Kaihsu, Kaiwhakahaere, Kala25, Kanabekobaton, Karimarie, Karl-Henner, Karmafist, Kathryn NicDhàna, Katieh5584, Kaveh, Kaybull, Kbdank71, Kbh3rd, Keilana, Keith Edkins, Keithdunwoody, KelvSYC, Kenaldinho10, Kernunnos, Kevin B12, Kevin9164, KevinTR, Kevinmon, Kevinzhermin, Keyrocks, Kfitzgib, Khoikhoi, Kidsrus, Kikinou, Kimchi.sg, King Toadsworth, King konger, King of Hearts (old account 2), Kingboyk, Kingjeff, Kingmahad121, Kinigi, Kixix, Kizara, Kizor, Kkm010, Kkornack, Klepto909, Kmccoy, Kneiphof, KnowledgeOfSelf, Kobbra, Kobebryantthejr, Konstable, Kornerkick29, Kosebamse, Kowtoo, Kpalion, Kri, Krich, Kruckenberg.1, KsprayDad, Kubigula, Kukini, Kungfuadam, Kungming2, Kuru, Kurykh, Kwekubo, Kwiki, Kylekyle1, Kylev1, KyraVixen, L Kensington, LSehy, Lacrimosus, Laenfant, Lance181, Landonbrowne, Lardman, Latics, Laughing Man, Laughingirl1515, Lazerburn33, Lazycouch2, Leafyplant, Leandrod, Lectonar, Lee Gregz, LegolasGreenleaf, Leminy, Lemonus, Leon7, Lerdthenerd, Leszek Jańczuk, Liebitz, Liftarn, Lightdarkness, Lightmouse, Lights, Lilcou123, Lilyana, Lindberg, Linkspamremover, Linuxerist, Lion King, Littlechip90, Lkkn, Llcoolspence, Loboxx36, Lofike, Logan, Loganbking, LonelyMarble, Lord Hawk, Lord Marco, Lord Voldemort, LordRM, LordSimonofShropshire, Lordkazan, Loren36, Lost4eva, Lotje, Lowercase, Lowzeewee, Lpw, LuFisto, Lucy-marie, Ludraman, LukeSurl, Lumpy joe108, Luna Santin, Lupin, M baptiste, MECU, MER-C, MJCdetroit, MK8, MNAdam, MZMcBride, Mac, Mac Gille Domhnaich, Mac12, MacGyverMagic, Mad sam, MadGeographer, Maday94, Madchester, Maddox, Madw, Maestro25, Magic in the night, Magister Mathematicae, Magooch2.0, Mah favourite, Mahahahaneapneap, Mahanga, Maihu don, Maitch, Majorly, Malhonen, Malo, Malpass93, Mandel, Maniacgeorge, Maniwar, Manuel11223, Manutd 12345, MapsMan, Marc Venot, Marcika, Marco.spiro, Mareino, Marek69, Marianocecowski, Mark, Mark272, MarkA12, Marrilpet, Marshman, MartinHarper, MartinVillafuerte85, Martingio15, Martyn Smith, Marudubshinki, Master Of Ninja, Masterpjz9, Materialscientist, Mateus RM, Matgggggg, Mathnarg, Matiasmoreno, Matt Yeager, Matt r kelly, Matthew R Dunn, Matthewfreile, Mattisse, Matty2002, Mauro100, Mav, Maveric56, Maw, Maxamegalon2000, Maxim, Maximaximax, Maxtin, Mayumashu, Mbecker, McDogm, McKennaMan929, Mcdeans, Mdr2375, Meb83, Meelar, Megan1967, Mendor, Meow1234, Merrettrg01, Methnor, Metropolitan90, Mets501, MetsFan76, Mgaigg, Mglovesfun, Michael (vandal), Michael Hardy, Michael Hawkins, Michael Hinrichs, Michael Johnson, Michael Zimmermann, Michael riber jorgensen, Michael-Zero, MickMacNee, MickWest, Midgrid, Miguel.mateo, Mike Rosoft, Mike jones gyeah, Mike1, MikeDog94, Mikethechicken, Mikm, Miles Blues, Minesweeper, Minna Sora no Shita, Mintguy, Mirage5000, MisfitToys, Mistakefinder, Mistamagic28, MisterSheik, Misure poo poo, Misza13, Mitsuhirato, Mjfc, Mkamensek, Mmoneypenny, Mmortal03, Mnpeter, MoRsE, Mochachocca, Moeron, Moeyman, Mohammad adil, Monarchius, Money Makers R Us, Monkbel, Monkeyman, Monkeyman11, Mono, Mopyu90, Moravice, Mormegil, Mothani90, Motley Crue Rocks, Mourn, Moyogo, Mr Chuckles, Mr. Bouncy, Mr. G. Williams, MrFish, MrH, MrJanitor1, MrTranscript, Mreult, Mroach12, Mrxcol, Ms2ger, Mshizzi, Mswake, Muchness, Muhammad Mahdi Karim, Mushroom, Mxalienraptor, Mxcatania, Myanw, Mybighead, Mysdaao, Mysekurity, N458jhk1, Nabla, Naddy, Nakon, Nanonic, Narco, Narsamson, Narssarssuaq, Nascar1996, Nath1012, Natjenko, NawlinWiki, Nawsum526, Ncmvocalist, Nebabc11, Nebu Pookins, Nedarb0, NeferSnoopy, Neil Leslie, Neiman002, New Vandal account!, New World Man, NewEnglandYankee, Newone, Nhilary, Nichalp, Nick, Nick Boulevard, Nick of nickness in Colorado, NickCT, Nickshanks, Night Gyr, Nihiltres, Nitaro02, Niteowlneils, Nmitbutcher, No Guru, NocturneNoir, Nodoremi, Noeticsage, Noirceuil, Nojika, Nolitafairytale, Nonagonal Spider, Nonforma, Norbutt2001, Northumbrian, Nosskyline, Nrbelex, Nscheffey, Nsh, Nuggets, Num1dgen, Number 57, Nzd, Nzfooty, OLDMAN, Obamafan70, Obli, Ocaasi, Ocrasaroon, Off!, Off2riorob, Ohconfucius, Ohheyyyy, Ohnoitsjamie, Oldelpaso, Oldhamlet, Olivier, Ollytedwards, Olorin28, Omengacarno07, Omglol, Omicronpersei8, On Thermonuclear War, One, OneManDown, OoberMick, Oogadabaga, Orangemaster, Ordinaria, Ortolan88, Ospalh, Othersider, Ouishoebean, Overlord pat, Ownage24, Oxfordwang, Ozbandit, PHDrillSergeant, PIO, Paavo273, Pacheto, Page Up, Pak21, Paleorthid, Palma234@sympatico.ca, Palmiped, Panarjedde, Papitasfritas, Parable1991, Paris 16, Park3r, Parksand, Parkwells, Pat Gibson, Pataya1, Patchamo123, Patrick, Patrick-br, Paul August, Pb30, Pdcook, Peanut4, PeeJay2K3, Persian Poet Gal, Perstar, Peruvianllama, Pespilaludo, Peter Eedy, Peter Isotalo, Peter S., PeterGrecian, Peterkoning, Peterstannard, Pewwer42, Phantomsnake, Phil Boswell, Philip Baird Shearer, PhilipO, PhilipR, Phillip J, Phobal, Phoenix2, PiRSquared17, Picapica, Pieguy48, PierceCheng, Pilif12p, Pilotboy5, Pilotguy, Pinirice65, Piontek, Pippu d'Angelo, Pit, Pizzaguy4378, Pladask, Plasticup, Plastikspork, Playak, Plm209, Poborak, PoeticVerse, Poindexter Propellerhead, Pokadoteliza, Pol098, Polarman, Poobslag, Poochy, Porqin, Portiere 101, Portillo, Poslanik, PotentialDanger, Poulsen, Powelldinho, Pparazorback, Ppntori, Pratj, PrestonH, Pretty Green, Prewitt81, PrimeCupEevee, Prodego, Pruneau, PseudoSudo, Psveindhoven, Psycho Kirby, Pusht, Python eggs, QAQUAU, Qrc2006, Quadell, Quae legit, QueenCake, Quilker, Quintillion, Quinxorin, QuizQuick, QwerpQwertus, R Lowry, RB972, RHaworth, RJSampson, RPlunk2853, RabidWalrus, Radio Guy, Raelx, Raf45Martinez, Rafaelamonteiro80, Rahuloof, Raichu, Rainjar, Rak-Tai, Ranjithsutari, Rapido, Raul654, Raven4x4x, Ravik, Ray Radlein, Ray7jd, Rd232, Rdikeman, Rdsmith4, Readeraml86, ReadingOldBoy, Recury, Red Director, Redcongocross, Reddi, Redrocketboy, Redshoeszeff, Redsox7897, Redvers, Redwolf24, Reeinstein, Refsworldlee, Regentagger, Reggy123, Reginmund, Regular Daddy, Renegadeviking, Rettetast, Rex the first, RexNL, Reyfan1710, Reywas92, Ricardo Moog, Ricardo monteiro, Rich Farmbrough, Richard Allen, Richard Harvey, Richard Rundle, Rick.G, RickK, Ricky81682, Rickyrab, Rjwilmsi, Rkstafford, Rlynagh-shannon, Rmachenw, Rmhermen, Robdurbar, RobertG, Roberta F., Robertgreer, Robversion1, Robwingfield, Rocket71048576, Rocketboy50, Roger491127, Rogerzilla, Romanm, Ronald Mexico, Rory096, Rosiethegreat, RoyBoy, Royalguard11, Royboycrashfan, Rreagan007, Rulesfan, Rx23xaexstlx, Ryan's mom, Ryan25, Rynne, Ryoissoawesome, Ryulong, S0ccerstud301, S0me l0ser, SAFCjl, SFC9394, SJK, SJP, SM, SMcCandlish, SNIyer12, SQGibbon, Sadettin, Sagz639, Salmon, Salt Yeung, Salvio giuliano, SalvoCalcio, Sam Hocevar, Sam Vimes, Samelchami, Sammalin, Sammyjames, Samsara, Samuel Blanning, SandyGeorgia, Sango123, Sangyerians, SaraBaugh, Sasajid, Sasquatch, Sausage948, Sbluen, Sbrools, Sceptre, SchfiftyThree, Schluum, Schrei, Scienter, Sciurinæ, Scottster03, Sdornan, Sean Whitton, Seanchelsea5, Searlewd, Sebasbronzini, Sebastiankessel, Seglea, Seidenstud, Serein (renamed because of SUL), Serminigo, Serpent-A, Serte, Sethlopez, Sfahey, Sgsilver, Shaddens ate denzel for brekky, Shadowjams, Shaidar cuebiyar, Shanes, Shannon bohle, Shirimasen, Shizhao, Shoemakerenator, Shojeeb, Shortenfs, Shotwell, Showersap12, Shrine of Fire, Shushruth, SidP, Sideshow Bob, Siebren, Sietse Snel, Silence, Silivrenion, SilkTork, Sillyfolkboy, Simba1409, SimonMayer, SimonP, SineWave, Sinteractive, Siqbal, Sir Cumsize, Sir Nicholas de Mimsy-Porpington, SirChan, SirGrant, SirJibby, Sirkad, Sixest, Sjakkalle, Sjorford, Sjö, Skh, Skinnyweed, SkullWeasel, Sky83, Skyler13, Slakr, Slow Graffiti, Sluj, Slumgum, Smart7167126716, Smaug123, Smithsterj, SmthManly, Snarfsnarf, Snipeboy09, Snori, SoCalSuperEagle, SoLando, Soaringbear, Sobolewski, Soccer buff, Soccer plyr66, Soccer219, SoccerNews, Soccerdude, Soccereditor, Soccerkick8, Soccerking11, Soccerman10103, Soccershoes1, Socialsoccer.com, Sofie310, SofiePedersen, Sonjaaa, Soulresin, SouthernNights, SpNeo, Spaniard78, SparqMan, Speed Air Man, Speedy McG, Spencer, SpencerTC, Speshel k, Spewmaster, SpiceMan, Spike Wilbury, Spitzerman, Spliffy, Splintax, Springeragh, SpuriousQ, Spykesinmahshoe, Sq178pv, Squall88, Srose, Ssilvers, St.daniel, Stalfur, Stanrosander, Stanza13, Starcircloco, Starx, Statistic94, Steel, Steers82, Steinan3, Stephen G. Brown, Stephen Parnell, Stephenb, Stepshep, SteveSims, Stevekeiretsu, Stevenhonig, Stevertigo, Stevey7788, Stevo1000, Stockdiver, Stop Climate Change, Struway, Struway2, Stu.W UK, Stui, Stylus Happenstance, Stymphal, Suhalbansal, Suisui, Summerford40, SupaStarGirl, Supadawg, Supplementary, Svick, Swainstonation, Swanyk, Symane, Symon, SynergyBlades, Szater, TFCforever, THUGCHILDz, TLE, TNB774, TRBlom, TSO1D, Taamu, Tad Lincoln, Taemyr, Tainter, TakuyaMurata, Tameamseo, Tanaats, Tancred, Tangerines, Tannin, Tanv91, Tara969, Taroaldo, Tasc, Tata11, Tavix, Tawker, Taylorr, Tbhotch, TeaDrinker, Teapeat, Tedcurly, Tellyaddict, TexMurphy, Thaurisil, The 984, The Anome, The Big C, The Font, The Gnome, The Halo, The Haunted Angel, The Rambling Man, The sock that should not be, The way, the truth, and the light, The wub, TheAmericanizator, TheGrappler, TheProject, Theda, Thefullback, Themodelcitizen, Thenotoriousadin, Therandomthing, Therightclique, Thesoccerjunky4, Thing that goes on feet, Thistle71190, Thryduulf, Thumperward, Thunderboltz, Tiago Heitor, Tibre, TiffaF, TigerShark, Tim R, Timc, Timmc9106, Timrollpickering, Timwi, Tiresais, Titansfan7532, Titoxd, Toby Woodwark, Tocino, Tom harrison, Tom-3124, Tom-3124(back again), TomCat4680, TomPhil, TomasBat, Tony1, TonySt, Tonywalton, Toondude, TootinDaylight, Totsie07, Tpbradbury, Travelbird, Tree Biting Conspiracy, Treed, Trevor MacInnis, Trieste, Trixxy, Trontonian, Trosk, Trouserswonky, Troutrooper, Trovatore, Trusilver, TurboGUY, Tvaughn05, TwoOneTwo, Tyciol, Tyomitch, Uannis, UberCryxic, Ughs, Ultimus, Ultratomio, Un chien andalou, Une fette, Unexplained, Unibond, UnicornTapestry, Unreal7, Uranium grenade, UrbanNerd, Uris, Urzadek, Usergreatpower, Utcursch, Utopial, V111P, VMohanty, Vanjagenije, Vanky, Varitek, Vary, Veed, Vega84, VegaDark, Veinor, Venu62, Vf7993, Viajero, Vidshow, Vikreykja, Vilcxjo, VinceBowdren, Violetriga, Viridae, Viriditas, Vivio Testarossa, Voyagerfan5761, Vrenator, VsD, Vzbs34, W2ch00, WATP, WAvegetarian, WFCforLife, Wackywace, Waggers, Wallerstein, Warfvinge, Warp457, Waseh123321, Wathiik, Wavelength, Wayward, Weregerbil, West coast, Westendgirl, Whall2004, Whatupnathan, Where, Whisky drinker, WhisperToMe, Whouk, Wi-king, Wiki Raja, Wiki alf, Wikibofh, Wikieditor06, Wikien2009, Wikitanvir, Wildnox, Wildplayer61, Will Beback Auto, Willbellum, Willis, Willy on Wheels, Willy turner, Wingsandsword, Winhunter, Winston365, Wipe, Wknight94, Wmahan, WojPob, Wolfmankurd, WoodenTaco, Woody, Woohookitty, Wrathchild, Wrp103, Wstitans11, Wtmitchell, Wtwilson3, Wutizevrybudylookingat?, Ww2censor, X!, X201, Xanthoxyl, Xaosflux, Xezbeth, Xhack, Xiaodai, Xiner, Xinit, Xornok, Xtra, Xzyilum, Y, Yarnalgo, Yaz0r, Yclept:Berr, Yeahsoo, Yekrats, YellowMonkey, Yoenit, Yonatan, Youndbuckerz, Your soccer boy, Yousou, Ysangkok, Yuckfoo, YuffieTheBear, Zachary Allen Berg, Zahid Abdassabur, Zanimum, Zaphod Beeblebrox, Zaslav, Zephyr21, ZimZalaBim, Zizouthecat, Zocky, Zolstijers, Zreeon, Zundark, Zytroft, Zzmonty, Zzuuzz, Zzyzx11, ²¹², Ævar Arnfjörð Bjarmason, Александър, Саша Стефановић, ||ممیءرری, فرش, ا دلين, 3260 anonymous edits

Image Sources, Licenses and Contributors

File:Belfast_Telegraph_Championship_logo.jpg *Source*: http://en.wikipedia.org/w/index.php?title=File:Belfast_Telegraph_Championship_logo.jpg *License*: unknown *Contributors*: Malpass93, Reddev87
File:Ulster banner.svg *Source*: http://en.wikipedia.org/w/index.php?title=File:Ulster_banner.svg *License*: unknown *Contributors*: Jean-Pierre Demailly
File:Soccerball current event.svg *Source*: http://en.wikipedia.org/w/index.php?title=File:Soccerball_current_event.svg *License*: unknown *Contributors*: User:Anomie, User:Davidgothberg, User:Pumbaa80
File:Inver Park, Larne (1) - geograph.org.uk - 2314259.jpg *Source*: http://en.wikipedia.org/w/index.php?title=File:Inver_Park,_Larne_(1)_-_geograph.org.uk_-_2314259.jpg *License*: unknown *Contributors*: Albert Bridge
File:Flag of Ireland.svg *Source*: http://en.wikipedia.org/w/index.php?title=File:Flag_of_Ireland.svg *License*: unknown *Contributors*: User:SKopp
File:Flag of Scotland.svg *Source*: http://en.wikipedia.org/w/index.php?title=File:Flag_of_Scotland.svg *License*: unknown *Contributors*: User:Kbolino
File:Wayne_County_Michigan_Incorporated_and_Unincorporated_areas_Allen_Park_highlighted.svg *Source*: http://en.wikipedia.org/w/index.php?title=File:Wayne_County_Michigan_Incorporated_and_Unincorporated_areas_Allen_Park_highlighted.svg *License*: unknown *Contributors*: Arkyan
Image:Uniroyal tire.jpg *Source*: http://en.wikipedia.org/w/index.php?title=File:Uniroyal_tire.jpg *License*: unknown *Contributors*: James Marvin Phelps from USA
File:Bridge over Six Mile Water, Antrim.jpg *Source*: http://en.wikipedia.org/w/index.php?title=File:Bridge_over_Six_Mile_Water,_Antrim.jpg *License*: unknown *Contributors*: Ardfern, Rodhullandemu, Прон
file:Northern Ireland map - July 2007.png *Source*: http://en.wikipedia.org/w/index.php?title=File:Northern_Ireland_map_-_July_2007.png *License*: unknown *Contributors*: Asarlaí, Joey-das-WBF, Jza84, Rathgarrr, Revolus, Shizhao, 1 anonymous edits
File:Red pog.svg *Source*: http://en.wikipedia.org/w/index.php?title=File:Red_pog.svg *License*: unknown *Contributors*: Anomie
File:RoundTowerAntrim3.jpg *Source*: http://en.wikipedia.org/w/index.php?title=File:RoundTowerAntrim3.jpg *License*: unknown *Contributors*: William Mervyn Lawrence (1840-1932)
File:Antrim Masonic Hall - geograph.org.uk - 76301.jpg *Source*: http://en.wikipedia.org/w/index.php?title=File:Antrim_Masonic_Hall_-_geograph.org.uk_-_76301.jpg *License*: unknown *Contributors*: Ardfern
File:Junction One Retail Park (2), August 2009.JPG *Source*: http://en.wikipedia.org/w/index.php?title=File:Junction_One_Retail_Park_(2),_August_2009.JPG *License*: unknown *Contributors*: User:Ardfern
File:CarlingPremiershipbig.jpg *Source*: http://en.wikipedia.org/w/index.php?title=File:CarlingPremiershipbig.jpg *License*: unknown *Contributors*: Malpass93, Mooretwin
File:Flag of Albania.svg *Source*: http://en.wikipedia.org/w/index.php?title=File:Flag_of_Albania.svg *License*: unknown *Contributors*: User:Dbenbenn
File:Flag of Malta.svg *Source*: http://en.wikipedia.org/w/index.php?title=File:Flag_of_Malta.svg *License*: unknown *Contributors*: Alkari, Fry1989, Gabbe, Homo lupus, Klemen Kocjancic, Liftarn, Mattes, Meno25, Nightstallion, Peeperman, Pumbaa80, Ratatosk, Rodejong, Zscout370, 4 anonymous edits
File:Flag of Wales 2.svg *Source*: http://en.wikipedia.org/w/index.php?title=File:Flag_of_Wales_2.svg *License*: unknown *Contributors*: AlexD, Cecil, Dbenbenn, Duduziq, F. F. Fjodor, FruitMonkey, Fry1989, Homo lupus, Iago4096, Pumbaa80, Red devil 666, Srtxg, Tha real, Torstein, Vernanimalcula, Vzb83, Wouterhagens, 7 anonymous edits
File:Flag of Estonia.svg *Source*: http://en.wikipedia.org/w/index.php?title=File:Flag_of_Estonia.svg *License*: unknown *Contributors*: User:PeepP, User:SKopp
file:football iu 1996.jpg *Source*: http://en.wikipedia.org/w/index.php?title=File:Football_iu_1996.jpg *License*: unknown *Contributors*: Attenboroughp, Avicennais, Badmachine, Beao, Brucelee, Circeus, Danielk2, Davepape, Herbythyme, J 1982, Juiced lemon, Jusjih, MGA73, Man vyi, Martin H., Ranveig, Rdikeman, Rjt170977, Samleeproductions, Spellcast, Thumperward, Túrelio, Wouterhagens, 23 anonymous edits
File:U20-WorldCup2007-Okotie-Onka edit2.jpg *Source*: http://en.wikipedia.org/w/index.php?title=File:U20-WorldCup2007-Okotie-Onka_edit2.jpg *License*: unknown *Contributors*: User:Fir0002, User:Nwiebe
File:Soccer goalkeeper.jpg *Source*: http://en.wikipedia.org/w/index.php?title=File:Soccer_goalkeeper.jpg *License*: unknown *Contributors*: U.S. Air Force photo by Master Sgt. Lance Cheung
File:Fußballgeschichte (1872).jpg *Source*: http://en.wikipedia.org/w/index.php?title=File:Fußballgeschichte_(1872).jpg *License*: unknown *Contributors*: Daemonic Kangaroo, Infrogmation, Juiced lemon, Kinigi, Maksim, Man vyi, Pepito, 3 anonymous edits
File:1stRoyalEngineers.png *Source*: http://en.wikipedia.org/w/index.php?title=File:1stRoyalEngineers.png *License*: unknown *Contributors*: Ffahm, Responsible?
File:Football pitch metric.svg *Source*: http://en.wikipedia.org/w/index.php?title=File:Football_pitch_metric.svg *License*: unknown *Contributors*: User:NielsF
File:Shunsuke1 20080622.jpg *Source*: http://en.wikipedia.org/w/index.php?title=File:Shunsuke1_20080622.jpg *License*: unknown *Contributors*: User:Neier
Image:Yellow card.svg *Source*: http://en.wikipedia.org/w/index.php?title=File:Yellow_card.svg *License*: unknown *Contributors*: User:ed_g2s
Image:Red card.svg *Source*: http://en.wikipedia.org/w/index.php?title=File:Red_card.svg *License*: unknown *Contributors*: User:ed_g2s
File:Ryan Valentine scores.jpg *Source*: http://en.wikipedia.org/w/index.php?title=File:Ryan_Valentine_scores.jpg *License*: unknown *Contributors*: User:Markbarnes
File:Mecz Polska - Armenia 04 ssj 20070328.jpg *Source*: http://en.wikipedia.org/w/index.php?title=File:Mecz_Polska_-_Armenia_04_ssj_20070328.jpg *License*: unknown *Contributors*: User:Staszek_Szybki_Jest
File:Cesc Fàbregas Anderson.jpg *Source*: http://en.wikipedia.org/w/index.php?title=File:Cesc_Fàbregas_Anderson.jpg *License*: unknown *Contributors*: Gordon Flood

GNU Free Documentation License Version 1.2, November 2002 Copyright (C) 2000,2001,2002 Free Software Foundation, Inc. 59 Temple Place, Suite 330, Boston, MA 02111-1307 USA Everyone is permitted to copy and distribute verbatim copies of this license document, but changing it is not allowed.

0. PREAMBLE

The purpose of this License is to make a manual, textbook, or other functional and useful document "free" in the sense of freedom: to assure everyone the effective freedom to copy and redistribute it, with or without modifying it, either commercially or noncommercially. Secondarily, this License preserves for the author and publisher a way to get credit for their work, while not being considered responsible for modifications made by others. This License is a kind of "copyleft", which means that derivative works of the document must themselves be free in the same sense. It complements the GNU General Public License, which is a copyleft license designed for free software. We have designed this License in order to use it for manuals for free software, because free software needs free documentation: a free program should come with manuals providing the same freedoms that the software does. But this License is not limited to software manuals; it can be used for any textual work, regardless of subject matter or whether it is published as a printed book. We recommend this License principally for works whose purpose is instruction or reference.

1. APPLICABILITY AND DEFINITIONS

This License applies to any manual or other work, in any medium, that contains a notice placed by the copyright holder saying it can be distributed under the terms of this License. Such a notice grants a world-wide, royalty-free license, unlimited in duration, to use that work under the conditions stated herein. The "Document", below, refers to any such manual or work. Any member of the public is a licensee, and is addressed as "you". You accept the license if you copy, modify or distribute the work in a way requiring permission under copyright law. A "Modified Version" of the Document means any work containing the Document or a portion of it, either copied verbatim, or with modifications and/or translated into another language. A "Secondary Section" is a named appendix or a front-matter section of the Document that deals exclusively with the relationship of the publishers or authors of the Document to the Document's overall subject (or to related matters) and contains nothing that could fall directly within that overall subject. (Thus, if the Document is in part a textbook of mathematics, a Secondary Section may not explain any mathematics.) The relationship could be a matter of historical connection with the subject or with related matters, or of legal, commercial, philosophical, ethical or political position regarding them. The "Invariant Sections" are certain Secondary Sections whose titles are designated, as being those of Invariant Sections, in the notice that says that the Document is released under this License. If a section does not fit the above definition of Secondary then it is not allowed to be designated as Invariant. The Document may contain zero Invariant Sections. If the Document does not identify any Invariant Sections then there are none. The "Cover Texts" are certain short passages of text that are listed, as Front-Cover Texts or Back-Cover Texts, in the notice that says that the Document is released under this License. A Front-Cover Text may be at most 5 words, and a Back-Cover Text may be at most 25 words. A "Transparent" copy of the Document means a machine-readable copy, represented in a format whose specification is available to the general public, that is suitable for revising the document straightforwardly with generic text editors or (for images composed of pixels) generic paint programs or (for drawings) some widely available drawing editor, and that is suitable for input to text formatters or for automatic translation to a variety of formats suitable for input to text formatters. A copy made in an otherwise Transparent file format whose markup, or absence of markup, has been arranged to thwart or discourage subsequent modification by readers is not Transparent. An image format is not Transparent if used for any substantial amount of text. A copy that is not "Transparent" is called "Opaque". Examples of suitable formats for Transparent copies include plain ASCII without markup, Texinfo input format, LaTeX input format, SGML or XML using a publicly available DTD, and standard-conforming simple HTML, PostScript or PDF designed for human modification. Examples of transparent image formats include PNG, XCF and JPG. Opaque formats include proprietary formats that can be read and edited only by proprietary word processors, SGML or XML for which the DTD and/or processing tools are not generally available, and the machine-generated HTML, PostScript or PDF produced by some word processors for output purposes only. The "Title Page" means, for a printed book, the title page itself, plus such following pages as are needed to hold, legibly, the material this License requires to appear in the title page. For works in formats which do not have any title page as such, "Title Page" means the text near the most prominent appearance of the work's title, preceding the beginning of the body of the text. A section "Entitled XYZ" means a named subunit of the Document whose title either is precisely XYZ or contains XYZ in parentheses following text that translates XYZ in another language. (Here XYZ stands for a specific section name mentioned below, such as "Acknowledgements", "Dedications", "Endorsements", or "History".) To "Preserve the Title" of such a section when you modify the Document means that it remains a section "Entitled XYZ" according to this definition. The Document may include Warranty Disclaimers next to the notice which states that this License applies to the Document. These Warranty Disclaimers are considered to be included by reference in this License, but only as regards disclaiming warranties: any other implication that these Warranty Disclaimers may have is void and has no effect on the meaning of this License.

2. VERBATIM COPYING

You may copy and distribute the Document in any medium, either commercially or noncommercially, provided that this License, the copyright notices, and the license notice saying this License applies to the Document are reproduced in all copies, and that you add no other conditions whatsoever to those of this License. You may not use technical measures to obstruct or control the reading or further copying of the copies you make or distribute. However, you may accept compensation in exchange for copies. If you distribute a large enough number of copies you must also follow the conditions in section 3. You may also lend copies, under the same conditions stated above, and you may publicly display copies.

3. COPYING IN QUANTITY

If you publish printed copies (or copies in media that commonly have printed covers) of the Document, numbering more than 100, and the Document's license notice requires Cover Texts, you must enclose the copies in covers that carry, clearly and legibly, all these Cover Texts: Front-Cover Texts on the front cover, and Back-Cover Texts on the back cover. Both covers must also clearly and legibly identify you as the publisher of these copies. The front cover must present the full title with all words of the title equally prominent and visible. You may add other material on the covers in addition. Copying with changes limited to the covers, as long as they preserve the title of the Document and satisfy these conditions, can be treated as verbatim copying in other respects. If the required texts for either cover are too voluminous to fit legibly, you should put the first ones listed (as many as fit reasonably) on the actual cover, and continue the rest onto adjacent pages. If you publish or distribute Opaque copies of the Document numbering more than 100, you must either include a machine-readable Transparent copy along with each Opaque copy, or state in or with each Opaque copy a computer-network location from which the general network-using public has access to download using public-standard network protocols a complete Transparent copy of the Document, free of added material. If you use the latter option, you must take reasonably prudent steps, when you begin distribution of Opaque copies in quantity, to ensure that this Transparent copy will remain thus accessible at the stated location until at least one year after the last time you distribute an Opaque copy (directly or through your agents or retailers) of that edition to the public. It is requested, but not required, that you contact the authors of the Document well before redistributing any large number of copies, to give them a chance to provide you with an updated version of the Document.

4. MODIFICATIONS

You may copy and distribute a Modified Version of the Document under the conditions of sections 2 and 3 above, provided that you release the Modified Version under precisely this License, with the Modified Version filling the role of the Document, thus licensing distribution and modification of the Modified Version to whoever possesses a copy of it. In addition, you must do these things in the Modified Version: A. Use in the Title Page (and on the covers, if any) a title distinct from that of the Document, and from those of previous versions (which should, if there were any, be listed in the History section of the Document). You may use the same title as a previous version if the original publisher of that version gives permission. B. List on the Title Page, as authors, one or more persons or entities responsible for authorship of the modifications in the Modified Version, together with at least five of the principal authors of the Document (all of its principal authors, if it has fewer than five), unless they release you from this requirement. C. State on the Title page the name of the publisher of the Modified Version, as the publisher. D. Preserve all the copyright notices of the Document. E. Add an appropriate copyright notice for your modifications adjacent to the other copyright notices. F. Include, immediately after the copyright notices, a license notice giving the public permission to use the Modified Version under the terms of this License, in the form shown in the Addendum below. G. Preserve in that license notice the full lists of Invariant Sections and required Cover Texts given in the Document's license notice. H. Include an unaltered copy of this License. I. Preserve the section Entitled "History", Preserve its Title, and add to it an item stating at least the title, year, new authors, and publisher of the Modified Version as given on the Title Page. If there is no section Entitled "History" in the Document, create one stating the title, year, authors, and publisher of the Document as given on its Title Page, then add an item describing the Modified Version as stated in the previous sentence. J. Preserve the network location, if any, given in the Document for public access to a Transparent copy of the Document, and likewise the network locations given in the Document for previous versions it was based on. These may be placed in the "History" section. You may omit a network location for a work that was published at least four years before the Document itself, or if the original publisher of the version it refers to gives permission. K. For any section Entitled "Acknowledgements" or "Dedications", Preserve the Title of the section, and preserve in the section all the substance and tone of each of the contributor acknowledgements and/or dedications given therein. L. Preserve all the Invariant Sections of the Document, unaltered in their text and in their titles. Section numbers or the equivalent are not considered part of the section titles. M. Delete any section Entitled "Endorsements". Such a section may not be included in the Modified Version. N. Do not retitle any existing section to be Entitled "Endorsements" or to conflict in title with any Invariant Section. O. Preserve any Warranty Disclaimers. If the Modified Version includes new front-matter sections or appendices that qualify as Secondary Sections and contain no material copied from the Document, you may at your option designate some or all of these sections as invariant. To do this, add their titles to the list of Invariant Sections in the Modified Version's license notice. These titles must be distinct from any other section titles. You may add a section Entitled "Endorsements", provided it contains nothing but endorsements of your Modified Version by various parties--for example, statements of peer review or that the text has been approved by an organization as the authoritative definition of a standard. You may add a passage of up to five words as a Front-Cover Text, and a passage of up to 25 words as a Back-Cover Text, to the end of the list of Cover Texts in the Modified Version. Only one passage of Front-Cover Text and one of Back-Cover Text may be added by (or through arrangements made by) any one entity. If the Document already includes a cover text for the same cover, previously added by you or by arrangement made by the same entity you are acting on behalf of, you may not add another; but you may replace the old one, on explicit permission from the previous publisher that added the old one. The author(s) and publisher(s) of the Document do not by this License give permission to use their names for publicity for or to assert or imply endorsement of any Modified Version.

5. COMBINING DOCUMENTS

You may combine the Document with other documents released under this License, under the terms defined in section 4 above for modified versions, provided that you include in the combination all of the Invariant Sections of all of the original documents, unmodified, and list them all as Invariant Sections of your combined work in its license notice, and that you preserve all their Warranty Disclaimers. The combined work need only contain one copy of this License, and multiple identical Invariant Sections may be replaced with a single copy. If there are multiple Invariant Sections with the same name but different contents, make the title of each such section unique by adding at the end of it, in parentheses, the name of the original author or publisher of that section if known, or else a unique number. Make the same adjustment to the section titles in the list of Invariant Sections in the license notice of the combined work. In the combination, you must combine any sections Entitled "History" in the various original documents, forming one section Entitled "History"; likewise combine any sections Entitled "Acknowledgements", and any sections Entitled "Dedications". You must delete all sections Entitled "Endorsements".

6. COLLECTIONS OF DOCUMENTS

You may make a collection consisting of the Document and other documents released under this License, and replace the individual copies of this License in the various documents with a single copy that is included in the collection, provided that you follow the rules of this License for verbatim copying of each of the documents in all other respects. You may extract a single document from such a collection, and distribute it individually under this License, provided you insert a copy of this License into the extracted document, and follow this License in all other respects regarding verbatim copying of that document.

7. AGGREGATION WITH INDEPENDENT WORKS

A compilation of the Document or its derivatives with other separate and independent documents or works, in or on a volume of a storage or distribution medium, is called an "aggregate" if the copyright resulting from the compilation is not used to limit the legal rights of the compilation's users beyond what the individual works permit. When the Document is included in an aggregate, this License does not apply to the other works in the aggregate which are not themselves derivative works of the Document. If the Cover Text requirement of section 3 is applicable to these copies of the Document, then if the Document is less than one half of the entire aggregate, the Document's Cover Texts may be placed on covers that bracket the Document within the aggregate, or the electronic equivalent of covers if the Document is in electronic form. Otherwise they must appear on printed covers that bracket the whole aggregate.

8. TRANSLATION

Translation is considered a kind of modification, so you may distribute translations of the Document under the terms of section 4. Replacing Invariant Sections with translations requires special permission from their copyright holders, but you may include translations of some or all Invariant Sections in addition to the original versions of these Invariant Sections. You may include a translation of this License, and all the license notices in the Document, and any Warranty Disclaimers, provided that you also include the original English version of this License and the original versions of those notices and disclaimers. In case of a disagreement between the translation and the original version of this License or a notice or disclaimer, the original version will prevail. If a section in the Document is Entitled "Acknowledgements", "Dedications", or "History", the requirement (section 4) to Preserve its Title (section 1) will typically require changing the actual title.

9. TERMINATION

You may not copy, modify, sublicense, or distribute the Document except as expressly provided for under this License. Any other attempt to copy, modify, sublicense or distribute the Document is void, and will automatically terminate your rights under this License. However, parties who have received copies, or rights, from you under this License will not have their licenses terminated so long as such parties remain in full compliance.

10. FUTURE REVISIONS OF THIS LICENSE

The Free Software Foundation may publish new, revised versions of the GNU Free Documentation License from time to time. Such new versions will be similar in spirit to the present version, but may differ in detail to address new problems or concerns. See http://www.gnu.org/copyleft/. Each version of the License is given a distinguishing version number. If the Document specifies that a particular numbered version of this License "or any later version" applies to it, you have the option of following the terms and conditions either of that specified version or of any later version that has been published (not as a draft) by the Free Software Foundation. If the Document does not specify a version number of this License, you may choose any version ever published (not as a draft) by the Free Software Foundation. ADDENDUM: How to use this License for your documents To use this License in a document you have written, include a copy of the License in the document and put the following copyright and license notices just after the title page: Copyright (c) YEAR YOUR NAME. Permission is granted to copy, distribute and/or modify this document under the terms of the GNU Free Documentation License, Version 1.2 or any later version published by the Free Software Foundation; with no Invariant Sections, no Front-Cover Texts, and no Back-Cover Texts. A copy of the license is included in the section entitled "GNU Free Documentation License". If you have Invariant Sections, Front-Cover Texts and Back-Cover Texts, replace the "with...Texts." line with this: with the Invariant Sections being LIST THEIR TITLES, with the Front-Cover Texts being LIST, and with the Back-Cover Texts being LIST. If you have Invariant Sections without Cover Texts, or some other combination of the three, merge those two alternatives to suit the situation. If your document contains nontrivial examples of program code, we recommend releasing these examples in parallel under your choice of free software license, such as the GNU General Public License, to permit their use in free software.

Lightning Source UK Ltd.
Milton Keynes UK
UKOW05f0330030813

214801UK00001B/276/P